NOTES *on* DEMOCRACY

NOTES *on* DEMOCRACY

H.L. MENCKEN

A NEW EDITION

Introduction and Annotations by
MARION ELIZABETH RODGERS

Afterword by
ANTHONY LEWIS

DISSIDENT BOOKS
New York

Published by arrangement with Alfred A. Knopf,
a division of Random House, Inc.

For publicity, sales and editorial information contact
Nicholas Towasser (646) 422-3100

Dissident Books
P.O. Box 20547
New York, New York 10021
Email: publisher@dissidentbooks.com
www.dissidentbooks.com

Library of Congress Cataloging-in-Publication Data

Mencken, H. L. (Henry Louis), 1880-1956.
Notes on democracy / by H.L. Mencken. — A new edition / with introduction and annotations by Marion Elizabeth Rodgers.
p. cm.
Includes bibliographical references.
LCCN 2007920465
ISBN-13: 978-0-9773788-1-4
ISBN-10: 0-9773788-1-0
1. Democracy. I. Rodgers, Marion Elizabeth. II. Title.
JC423.M46 2008 321.8 QBI07-600050

Book design and type formatting by Bernard Schleifer
Manufactured in the United States of America

Contents

Introduction

In 1926, when *Notes on Democracy* was published, Walter Lippmann praised H. L. Mencken as "the most powerful personal influence upon this whole generation of educated people," calling him a force that had exerted "an extraordinarily cleansing and vitalizing effect."[1] Mencken indicted the platitudes of American life with indignation, ferocity, and humor, even glee. As critic Van Wyck Brooks noted, "there was no doubt that this wit, along with the point of view behind it, had liberated American thinking and feeling to an extraordinary degree."[2]

Today, the opposite of that exalted opinion prevails. Last year, when the Estate for H. L. Mencken and Dissident Books approached me to write the introduction and annotations to this book, Mencken was still castigated as un-American, "anti-democractic," even "a near anarchist."[3] His independent and realistic thought is sternly censured; in more liberated circles, it is simply regarded with unease. When every phrase must be examined for political correctness, many find it impossible to enjoy Mencken without apology.

Elsewhere in the world, Mencken remains a touchstone to American culture. He is recognized as an influential literary critic and appreciated as the preeminent iconoclastic observer of the American scene at a time when newspapers were regarded as the principal forum of public debate. Of that era, H. L. Mencken is among the few journalists whose work and reputation have best stood the test of time.

The truth is Mencken defies categorization. He was a complex man of many contradictions. He made disparaging remarks about blacks and Jews in his diary, yet crusaded against the Ku Klux Klan, lobbied with the NAACP for an anti-lynching bill, and urged the Roosevelt administration to open America's doors to Jews fleeing Nazi Germany. Mencken himself sponsored refugee families. He publicly argued for the cultural superiority of Germany during both World Wars and the concept of monarchy held an attraction for him, yet he devoted most of his life to a multi-volume study of the American language, a tribute to the classes and races that created it and a declaration of independence from Europe. Without question, his faults have justifiably aroused feelings of betrayal and disappointment in those who have blindly set him up as an idol. They have also been the source of arousing blatant misinterpretation.

Nonetheless, the many facets of Mencken's character were tied together by a single principle: "I am strongly in favor of liberty and I hate fraud."[4] This theme ran through all of his writings, whether literary criticism or political polemic. He was invariably amused when readers tried to peg him as from the political right or left. If anyone took the time to really examine his ideas, Mencken once joked, they would probably categorize him as a radical. When it came to assessing his own influence, he once wrote:

> If I have accomplished anything in this world it is this: that I have made life measurably more bearable for the civilized minority in America. The individuals of this minority are often surrounded by dark, dense seas of morons and so they tend to become hopeless. I have reason to believe that my books and other writings have given a little comfort to many such persons and even inspired some of them to revolt. I am glad of the comfort but the revolt doesn't interest me.[5]

Henry Louis Mencken was born on September 12, 1880, in Baltimore, Maryland. For two centuries the Menckens flourished in Leipzig, Germany, renowned as scholars, lawyers, and historians. The *Menckestrasse*, a road leading to the city center, is named for his ancestors. After landing in Baltimore in 1848, Henry's paternal grandfather prospered in the New World as a tobacco wholesaler. Mencken's father and uncle began their own cigar factory. Instead of following the family business, Henry longed to be a newspaper reporter. In 1898, his father's death freed him to enter what he called "the maddest, gladdest, damndest existence ever enjoyed by mortal youth."[6]

His rise was astronomical. As the youngest reporter on the *Baltimore Morning Herald,* he became its city editor when he was 23 years old; a year later he was its managing editor. After the *Herald* closed he switched to the *Baltimore Sun* in 1906, where he remained for the rest of his life, writing mostly for the newspaper's less reverential evening edition. By 1910 he was publishing a regular column, "The Free Lance," that became the precursor for his "Monday Articles," which appeared from 1920 to 1938. For most of his career his byline was synonymous with both the *Sun*'s morning and evening editions, except when his pro-German leanings forced him to leave in 1917 and again in 1941. Although Mencken was never syndicated, his caustic commentary against the shams of his day was quoted throughout this country and abroad. Mencken hoped to shock and stimulate his readers: if people did not agree with him that was fine. "I write because I like it," he insisted, "not because I want to convert anyone."[7]

Incredibly, for a man who felt like an outsider, who extolled German culture, Mencken was unabashedly American in his language, humor, and outlook. After World War I, when disillusioned Americans were sailing to Europe, Mencken had the choice to join them. Instead he remained. By the 1920s he was recognized as the nation's most influential critic, credited with freeing the country's literature from its Anglophilia to a uniquely American style. With George Jean Nathan, Mencken co-edited the *Smart Set* from 1914 to 1923. The following year they launched the *American Mercury,* which Mencken edited alone until 1933. Aimed at the "civilized minority," the *Mercury* was a mixture of politics, arts and sciences that examined American life. It was the first periodical run by a white editor to publish the work of black authors. It was the first mainstream, popular magazine to examine American folklore, race, medicine, architecture, music, and the immigrant press. Even its layout and typeset were unique. It revolutionized the magazine industry.[8] Mencken also wrote thirty books, ranging from studies of Nietzsche to a trilogy of light-hearted memoirs. Although *The American Language* is recognized as his most durable work, Mencken once mused that was only because it remained his least controversial. He considered himself a newspaperman with an unswerving commitment to freedom. His fame, as Alistair Cooke noted, was "rightly grounded on the vigor and noble indignation he brought to unpopular causes."[9] These included his stands against lynching, segregation, and censorship, sometimes taken at great risk, at a time when few took such stances.

"I know of no other man who believes in liberty more than I do," he said.[10] In this he was consistent. Although Mencken was against socialism in all its forms, he helped its advocates when their rights were denied.[11] He signed a petition calling for an end to the arrest of communists for expressing their opinions.[12] His philosophy, stated one critic, was "thoroughly American," the remnants of nineteenth-century liberal thought.[13]

Liberty was the only political right worth fighting for, Mencken declared. "I believe that any invasion of it is immensely dangerous to the commonweal—especially when that invasion is alleged to have a moral purpose. No conceivable moral purpose is higher than the right of the citizen to think whatever he pleases to think, and to carry on his private life without interference by others. If that right is taken away, then no moral system remains; all we have is a prison system. This begins to prevail in the United States."[14]

Notes on Democracy was the culmination of Mencken's thinking about democracy and the American character. Its origin was a series of articles which ran in the *Smart Set* from June through October 1913, written at a time when powerful forces were shaping the legal meaning of free speech, when many were denouncing the censorship of books and plays and the closing of the U.S. mail distribution to "questionable" material.[15]

The book was conceived as the first volume of a trilogy that would state his political, religious, and moral philosophy. In 1930, he published the second of the trilogy, *Treatise on the Gods;* in 1934, *Treatise on Right and Wrong.* But the actual writing of *Notes on Democracy,* said Mencken, turned out to be "a vexatious enterprise."[16] It garnered one of the lowest sales of his books: 6,100 copies sold, compared to 20,000 of *Treatise on the Gods.* It had only two printings, versus eleven by 1928 of *In Defense of Women.*[17]

Mencken began writing *Notes on Democracy* in 1923, but finding the time to organize it was difficult. At that period he launched the *American Mercury.* In July 1925 he began covering the Scopes trial. Upon his return to Baltimore other events made work "almost impossible."[18] That autumn he had to deal with the bankruptcy of his father's old firm, August Mencken & Bro., and his mother's illness and subsequent death. In the spring of 1926, Mencken was embroiled in the infamous "Hatrack" case, in which Boston authorities sought to ban for obscenity the April 1926 *American Mercury.* Because of so much personal and professional pressure, Mencken did not finish *Notes on Democracy* until June 1926, and only then, as he might have put it, by "sheer mule-power."[19]

As one critic has observed, *Notes on Democracy* remains "a significant contribution to popular libertarian debate . . . in eclipse for several decades."[20] The debate has finally reemerged as more Americans begin to express openly their dissatisfaction with the *status quo.* Until recently, heated discussion on matters including the hostility of evangelical Christians to science, the split between rural areas and the cities, the climate of censorship, prejudice and attacks on dissenters, overreaches of executive power, and matters of the role of the press during wartime seemed to exist only in the world of bloggers, who, like the Europeans, identify with Mencken's fiercely independent point of view. In Europe, it has been remarked that, "with just a little reworking," Mencken's observations on similar issues "would be appropriate to the opinion pages of U.S. newspapers today."[21]

Edmund Wilson, while praising *Notes on Democracy,* nevertheless thought it missed the cumulative force of a pamphlet by Jonathan Swift or George Bernard Shaw because it lacked the "entertainment of a closely reasoned argument to sustain the interest to the end."[22] The writer Rebecca West simply dismissed any comparisons to fellow countrymen Swift or Shaw. Instead she attempted to dispatch the American *provocateur* with this thrust: "No British author would have dared to put out a book so shallow, so slick, so innocent of argument and so empty of everything else."[23] Other critics, such as Henry Hazlitt, faulted it for its hyperbole, numerous inconsistencies, and grandiose generalizations.[24]

There were those, however, like Walter Lippmann and Henry Hazlitt, who reminded readers that one must not take Mencken's claims literally, but in a satirical sense, as one would with the work of a caricaturist, who brings to the fore "something which we immediately recognize to be penetrating and profoundly true."[25] This stance served Mencken very well. When *Notes on Democracy* was published, he Mencken was at the height of his fame, with more than 500 editorials on him printed in the U.S. No other contemporary critic was as well known in the colleges; for many, Mencken was "our great hero."[26] In the course of only a few hours, one reporter found seven riders with *Notes on Democracy* on the New York subway; in Central Park a flapper with bobbed hair was seen reading it to her boyfriend.[27]

Overseas, the Mencken cult had also reached new heights. Europeans had been the first to recognize his merits; his reputation abroad was as a literary phenomenon of the time. He was praised as the only modern critic who possessed a deep insight into American character. On the Continent, he was affectionately labeled "*l'enfant terrible de la critique americicaine.*"[28] Mencken's popularity extended to Britain, Africa, Australia, Asia, and South America. Perhaps the most enthusiastic reader of *Notes on Democracy* was Kaiser Wilhelm, former German emperor, then in exile in Holland. To this day, there is still a copy of *Notes on Democracy* in the emperor's small library at Doorn.[29]

Modern critics acknowledge that, for all of its limitations, any study of Mencken cannot ignore *Notes on Democracy*: it is the core of his philosophy.[30] Mencken divides his subject under three heads: "Democratic Man," "The Democratic State," and "Democracy and Liberty." He pays little attention to any alternative to democracy. Instead, there is more discussion about Democratic Man instead of democracy—one critic viewed it as *the* argument of the book.[31] Mencken defines society as a conflict between the superior man and the mob. His portrait of the mob-man, as Edmund Wilson remarked, is "an ideal monster, exactly like the Yahoo of Swift, and it has almost the same dreadful reality."[32] Mencken defines him as a man governed by emotions:

> Whenever he is confronted by a choice between two ideas, the one sound and the other not, he chooses, almost infallibly, and by a sort of pathological compulsion, the one that is not. Behind all the great tyrants and butchers of history he has marched with loud hosannas, but his hand is eternally against those who seek to liberate the spirit of the race . . . In two thousand years he has moved an inch: from the sports of the arena to the lynching party . . . What is worth knowing he doesn't know and doesn't want to know; what he knows is not true. The cardinal articles of his credo are the inventions of mountebanks; his heroes are mainly scoundrels.[33]

The inferior man absorbs delusions, Mencken argues. His mind is stocked with fear. Mencken continues: "The demagogues, *i.e.*, the professors of mob psychology, who flourish in democratic states are well aware of the fact, and make it the cornerstone of their exact and puissant science. Politics under democracy consists almost wholly of the discovery, chase and scotching of bugaboos."[34] The power of government is "concentrated upon throwing the plain people into a panic," in "melodramatic pursuits of horrendous monsters, most of them imaginary."[35]

All of the sound elements that exist in democracy—those that Mencken himself valued, such as equality before the law, free speech, and limitations of government—are abandoned in times of war. This personally became clear to him in 1917, when anti-German hysteria in this country reached such an epic scale that pacifists were silenced, jailed, and even killed; newspapers were censored, with penalties of $10,000 and 20 years in prison for any negative discussion of the war; and citizens joined private organizations to inform on fellow Americans. Adding to the hysteria were attacks against immigrants and German-Americans. The teaching of German was eliminated from public schools; German clubs disappeared; even food was renamed (*sauerkraut* became *liberty cabbage*). Americans were churned into a state of terror. Intolerance manifested itself to such a degree that fundamental liberties were unashamedly violated.[36]

Even with the return of peace, this frenzy extended into the 1920s, when many Americans began to blame their ills on a new bogeyman, the Soviet Bolshevik. In January 1920 alone, federal agents arrested 6,000 alleged communists in 33 cities across the nation.[37] Many were picked up without warrants or the right to contact lawyers or families. Scores of innocent people were clubbed or jailed for demonstrating publicly against the violation of the Bill of Rights. Few protested. "The average man doesn't want to be free," observed Mencken in *Notes*, "He simply wants to be safe."[38]

To Mencken, that helped explain the average man's tolerance of judicial fiats, however plainly they violate his fundamental rights. The chief mark of the inferior man, in Mencken's view, is that the values he holds most dear are false: patriotism, conformity, respectability. And while Mencken said he could understand patriotism, he also made it clear that there must be a genuine reason for it, and that the country should deserve it.

If Mencken seems bitter, he felt he had reason to be. Without precedent in American history, he argued, the government had hounded men and women in cynical violation of their constitutional rights. Instead of a democracy as laid out by the Founding Fathers, the country was hell-bent on blindly following leaders whose legacy included a "colossal waste of public money, the savage persecution of all opponents and critics of war, the open bribery of labor, the half-insane reviling of the enemy, the manufacture of false news, the knavish robbery of enemy civilians, the incessant spy hunts, the floating of public loans by a process of blackmail, the degradation of the Red Cross to partisan uses, the complete abandonment of all decency, decorum and self-respect."[39]

So who is the superior man in Mencken's view? Well, certainly not the monster that Mencken's detractors shrilly condemn, who define Mencken as an "anarchist" who "denounced democracy in the name of vitalism, eugenics and a caste system run by an elite of superior men."[40] For Mencken the superior man, regardless of race or social background, is simply the man of honor. By that he means an independent, enlightened citizen, predisposed toward liberty, on guard to keep his freedom from eroding under the pressure of self-styled patriots or unscrupulous politicians, who play upon the fears of people in troubled times. Such a man suffers in a democracy, Mencken argued: "He is beset on all sides, and every year sees an augmentation of his woes."[41]

The division between two groups of men, the "intelligent minority" and those whom Mencken referred to as "*homo boobensis*," was undoubtedly influenced by his study of Nietzsche. But to simply equate Mencken with "Nietzschean elitism" and include "German authoritarians, and eugenics" is taking the parallel much too far.[42] Mencken was not blind to German weaknesses, including as he put it, the "curious reverence for authority."[43] When eugenics became a worldwide movement, with its planning committees heavily involved in race betterment, Mencken found much to criticize.[44] As Mencken scholar Douglas C. Stenerson has pointed out, unlike Nietzsche, Mencken did not advocate "an oppressive regime acting under orders from the highest caste to keep the mob in check."[45] Mencken realized that democracy, even though it failed, had some useful gifts: equality before the law, which "had certain uses for human dignity."[46]

Mencken's standards for the superior "civilized man" recur throughout his *oeuvre*, not just in *Notes.* Decency, honor. and courage are values that he repeatedly touches upon. He hailed social Darwinist William Graham Sumner's concept of the Forgotten Man in the *American Mercury*'s first issue, describing him as "the normal, educated, well-disposed, unfrenzied, enlightened citizen of the middle minority," "sure of himself in the world," whose virtues include initiative, enterprise, self-reliance, courage, hard work, punctuality, and thrift.[47] Most importantly, he is a man of curiosity, receptive and tolerant of new ideas.

Notes on Democracy goes to great lengths to state how the inferior man suspects the man of honor. He lacks character, possessing only the eager desire to conform. At the same time, the inferior man recognizes his own shortcomings: he envies his betters because he realizes that the superior man possesses more courage. Thus, the inferior man is "incapable of bearing the pangs of liberty. They make him uncomfortable; they alarm him."[48] New ideas are unfamiliar, therefore threatening. Since the natural tendency of the inferior man is to oppose the whole progress of the world, he is a prohibitionist, anti-evolutionist, and a Puritan.

Mencken admired James Fenimore Cooper's 1838 study *The American Democrat.* Like Cooper, Mencken felt that democracy "warred upon the free functioning of genuinely superior men—how it kept them out of public life, and so forced them into silence and sterility, and robbed the commonwealth of their sense and decency."[49] Like the framers of the Constitution, who inveighed openly against the tyranny of the majority, Mencken felt that "the rule of the majority must tend toward a witless and malignant tyranny, anti-social in its motives and evil almost beyond endurance in its effects." These, said Mencken, "are the chief burdens of the democratic form of government."[50]

Mencken's concept forms the basis of Part II, "The Democratic State," where he skewers politicians in a democracy, who, "confronted by the dishonesty and stupidity of his master, the mob, tries to convince himself and all the rest of us that it is really full of . . . wisdom."[51] In other words, politicians are men who have sold their honor for their jobs. In a democracy, Mencken asserts, one cannot be honorable and a politician. "He is willing to embrace any issue, however idiotic, that will get him votes, and he is willing to sacrifice any principle, however sound, that will lose them for him."[52]

For Mencken, the question of whether democracy in the U.S. is really ideal is a moot point. Most of the so-called constitutional checks and balances have yielded at one time or another to the pressures of special interests. These groups, although small, are composed of "determined minorities," run by "ambitious individuals" who are "articulate and efficient," successful at turning their science of bamboozling and exploitation into "a delicate and lofty art."[53]

By way of example, Mencken cites the Supreme Court. No one familiar with its history, he argues, "need be told that its vast and singular power to curb legislation has always been exercised with one eye on the election returns."[54] Mencken marveled that "no candidate for the doctorate has ever written a realistic history of the American Department of Jusice, ironically so called."[55] "It is hard to recall an administration in which it was not the centre of grave scandal," writes Mencken, ". . . and at all times it has labored valiantly to nullify the guarantees of the Bill of Rights."[56] The anachronistic Electoral College, he continues, also makes for disproportionate representation in the way it has been set up. Such an argument is not new; as far back as 1816 many argued it should be abolished.

Mencken rushes through the third section, "Democracy and Liberty," though it is probably the most impassioned of all. If the tone seems strident, Mencken was convinced wartime statutes that violated First Amendment rights made democracy reach its *reductio ad absurdum*.[57] For him, the history of government has been a history of "successive usurpations. . . . No man would want to be President of the United States in strict accordance with the Constitution. There is no sense of power in merely executing laws; it comes from evading or augmenting them."[58]

At best, Mencken's hope for democracy was dim. At the end of his life, he realized that the only way it could survive or even be made "bearable" was by "developing and cherishing a class of men sufficiently honest and disinterested to challenge the prevailing quacks. No such class has ever appeared in strength in the United States."[59] To Mencken, this responsibility lay upon the press. "They constitute the only effective opposition," Mencken argued, "and one of their clearest duties is to keep a wary eye on the gentlemen who operate this great nation, and only too often slip into the assumption that they own it."[60] When newspapers fail in their duty, which Mencken snorted, "is usually, we are at the quacks' mercy."[61]

Mencken frequently railed against the American press. The editorial pages were "our grandest and gaudiest failure," he remarked. "Printing the news is only half the job. The rest is interpreting it, showing what it signifies, getting some sense and coherence into it."[62] For an examination of how war is packaged and promoted to a gullible public, go back to the files of American newspapers for 1914 and 1915, wherein a credulous press swallowed discrepancies, omissions, and distortions, and questioned the patriotism of anyone who did not buy the party line.[63] Mencken's pro-German leanings should not blind a reader to his sobering scrutiny of government propaganda and the role of the press. It was not for nothing that prompted Mencken to later remark, with characteristic damnation, that journalism was a profession of "public office seekers, title hunters, social pushers, dollar diddlers, mountebanks and cads."[64]

As Edmund Wilson shrewdly observed, *Notes on Democracy* is "another of Mencken's *Prejudices,* treated on a larger scale than the rest."[65] While not completely enthralled by the book, Wilson found it "quite remarkable as literature," defining it as a "prose poem . . . a sort of obverse of Whitman's *Leaves of Grass.*"[66]

Certainly *Notes on Democracy* was one of the most intensely felt of all of Mencken's books, one that Wilson asserted *ought* to be read. Although Mencken had been saying the same things for years, Wilson asserted they had never been said before "in so terse a language" or with such "satiric force," making the book "stirring and nearly tragic."[67] And he concluded:

> We may not always like the somewhat heavy-footed superman as we sometimes encounter him in Mencken's pages, and we may like him less when we encounter his embodiments in some of Mencken's admirers; but we must admit to have made the Americans recognize themselves in his super-boor and turn from the revelation in horror is no inconsiderable achievement.[68]

Mencken was, however, anything but a moralist—an attitude, he realized, that made him incomprehensible to most Americans. Toward the end of his life, he admitted: "I do not believe in democracy, but I am perfectly willing to admit that it provides the only really amusing form of government ever endured by mankind."[69]

If Mencken's flippancy strikes some as inadequate, then one should remember that his theses against democracy were, as he put it, those of a pathologist, not those of a therapist. "I have witnessed, in my day, the discovery, enthronement and subsequent collapse of a vast army of uplifters and world-savers, and am firmly convinced that all of them were mountebanks. . . . Nevertheless, we survive, and not only survive but flourish."[70] Therefore, Mencken insisted, "my view of my country is predominantly tolerant and amiable."[71] That Mencken encountered very little tolerance and amiability in return, as Mencken scholar Charles Fecher has pointed out, "only proved his point."[72]

In Europe, Mencken continues to have contemporary relevance, "as a testament to the necessity of reasoned dissent at a time of crisis and self-doubt."[73] Significantly, Mencken keeps cropping up; half a century after his death in 1956 he continues to "stir up the animals" with his common sense, lively wit, and the courage to say what he thought. To members of "the civilized minority," no matter what side of the political spectrum, he has lost none of his punch. As he observed in the *American Mercury:*

> Life may not be exactly pleasant, but it is at least not dull. Heave yourself into Hell today, and you may miss, tomorrow or next day, another Scopes trial, or another War to End War, or perchance a rich and buxom widow with all of her first husband's clothes. There are always more Hardings hatching. I advocate hanging on as long as possible.[74]

—Marion Elizabeth Rodgers
Washington, D.C., 2007

NOTES

1. Walter Lippmann, "H. L. Mencken," *Saturday Review of Literature*, December 11, 1926, pp. 413–14.

2. Van Wyck Brooks, "Mr. Mencken on Democracy," London *Times*, April 22, 1927.

3. Fred Siegel, "Mencken the Teuton," *The Weekly Standard*, January 30, 2006, p. 41.

4. H. L. Mencken, "Autobiographical Notes, 1925," p. 165. (The Mencken Collection, The Enoch Pratt Free Library).

5. Ibid., pp. 199–200.

6. H. L. Mencken, *Newspaper Days: 1899–1906* (New York: Alfred A. Knopf, 1943), p. ix.

7. Donald Ritchie, "H. L. Mencken, The Caustic Critic," *American Journalists* (New York: Oxford University Press, 1997), p. 191.

8. For further discussion see M. K. Singleton, *H. L. Mencken and the American Mercury Adventure* (Durham: Duke University Press, 1962).

9. Author interview with Alistair Cooke, May 2, 1992.

10. H. L. Mencken, "Autobiographical Notes, 1925," pp. 168–169.

11. Ibid.

12. "'Red Scare' Protest Issued By Liberals," *The New York Times*, May 19, 1930.

13. Ernest Boyd, *H. L. Mencken* (New York: McBride, 1925), p. 63.

14. H. L. Mencken, "Autobiographical Notes, 1925," p. 169.

15. H. L. Mencken, *My Life as Author and Editor,* edited by Jonathan Yardley (New York: Alfred A. Knopf, 1993), p. 39.

16. Ibid., p. 354.

17. H. L. Mencken to Norman Foerste, October 28, 1933. (The New York Public Library); "Royalty Statement," *Menckeniana*, Fall 1988, pp. 12–13.

18. H. L. Mencken, *Thirty-Five Years of Newspaper Work: A Memoir by H. L. Mencken,* edited by Fred Hobson, Vincent Fitzpatrick, and Bradford Jacobs (Baltimore: Johns Hopkins University Press, 1994), p. 154.

19. This was one of Mencken's typical phrases, once used to describe his completion of *Prejudices: Fourth Series.* Mencken to Sara Haardt, May 12, 1924. From: *Mencken and Sara: A Life in Letters,* edited by Marion Elizabeth Rodgers (New York: McGraw-Hill, 1987), p. 139.

20 George Hunka, "A Vast Field of Greased Poles: America and Americans in H. L. Mencken's *Notes on Democracy*," *Menckeniana*, Fall 1996, p. 6.

21. Conor Brady, "Warrior Armed With Words," *Irish Times,* April 8, 2006.

22. Edmund Wilson, "Mencken's Democratic Man," *The New Republic*, December 15, 1926, p. 111.

23. Rebecca West, "In Defense of a Democratic Idea," The New York *Herald Tribune*, November 14, 1926.

24. Henry Hazlitt, "Incurable Democracy: Mr. Mencken Lets Loose Another War Whoop," The New York *Sun*, October 30, 1926; "The Innocence of Father Mencken," *London Saturday Review*, February 19, 1927; G. K. Chesterton, "Our Notebook," *The Illustrated London News*, November 13, 1926, p. 918; Robert R. Hull, "Mencken on Democracy," *The Fortnightly Review*, March 15, 1927, pp. 129–130; R. K. Gooch, "Book Reviews," *Political Science Quarterly*, March 1927, pp. 443–444.

25. Walter Lippmann, "H. L. Mencken," *Saturday Review of Literature*, December 11, 1926, pp. 413–414; Henry Hazlitt, "Incurable Democracy..." The New York *Sun*, October 30, 1926.

26. *Sherwood Anderson's Memoirs: A Critical Edition*, edited by Ray Lewis White (Chapel Hill: University of North Carolina Press, 1969), p. 369.

27. Robert Garland, "Day by Day with Robert Garland," The Baltimore *Daily Post*, December 15, 1926.

28. Marion Elizabeth Rodgers, *Mencken: The American Iconoclast* (New York: Oxford University Press, 2005), p. 310.

29. Dr. Klaus Pohl to Dr. Helmut Winter, August 17, 2000. (Courtesy Dr. Helmut Winter to the author.)

30. Charles A. Fecher, *Mencken: A Study of His Thought* (New York: Alfred A. Knopf, 1978), p. 171; Terry Teachout, *The Skeptic: A Life of H. L. Mencken* (New York: Harper Collins, 2002), p. 229.

31. Anders Ivason, "Democratic Man, the Super Man and the Forgotten Man in H. L. Mencken's *Notes on Democracy*," *English Studies*, 1969 (50), p. 354.

32. Edmund Wilson, "Mencken's Democratic Man," *The New Republic*, December 15, 1926, p. 110.

33. H. L. Mencken, *Notes on Democracy* (New York: Alfred A. Knopf, 1926; New York: Dissident Books, 2008, pp. 65-66. (Page numbers refer to the present edition.)

34. Ibid., p. 40.

35. Ibid., pp. 43, 40.

36. For a discussion on these events, including notes, see Rodgers, *Mencken: The American Iconoclast*, pp. 175–220.

37. Ibid.

38. H. L. Mencken, *Notes on Democracy*, p. 117.

39. H. L. Mencken, "On Being an American," *Prejudices: Sixth Series* (New York: Alfred A. Knopf, 1927), p. 46.

40. Fred Siegel, "Mencken the Teuton," *The Weekly Standard*, January 30, 2006, p. 41.

41. H. L. Mencken, "Autobiographical Notes, 1925" p. 165.

42. Fred Siegel, "Mencken the Teuton," *The Weekly Standard,* January 30, 2006, p. 40.

43. H. L. Mencken, "The Prophet of the Superman," *The Smart Set,* March 1912, pp. 156–58.

44. H. L. Mencken, "On Eugenics," *Chicago Sunday Tribune*, May 15, 1927.

45. Douglas C. Stenerson, *Mencken: Iconoclast from Baltimore* (Chicago: University of Chicago Press, 1971), p. 121.

46. H. L. Mencken, *Minority Report* (New York: Alfred A. Knopf, 1956), p. 119; and H. L. Mencken, "Introduction," to James Fenimore Cooper, *The American Democrat* (New York: Alfred A. Knopf, 1931), xiii–xiv.

47. H. L. Mencken, "Editorial," the *American Mercury,* January 1924, p. 29.

48. H. L. Mencken, *Notes on Democracy,* p. 56.

49. H. L. Mencken, "Introduction," to James Fenimore Cooper, p. xiii.

50. Ibid.

51. Mencken, *Notes on Democracy*, p. 99.

52. Ibid., p. 91.

53. Ibid., pp. 74, 75.

54. Ibid., p. 83.

55. Ibid., p. 138.

56. Ibid..

57. Ibid., p. 89.

58. Ibid., p. 139.

59. H. L. Mencken, *Minority Report,* p. 125.

60. H. L. Mencken, "Speech at the Annual Luncheon of the Associated Press, New York, April 20, 1936," from "H. L. Mencken: Miscellaneous Speeches 1913–1938," pp. 48–53. (The Mencken Collection, The Enoch Pratt Free Library).

61. H. L. Mencken, *Minority Report,* p. 125.

62. H. L. Mencken, "Speech at the Annual Luncheon of the Associated Press . . . ," pp. 48–53.

63. For a discussion, with notes, see: Rodgers, *Mencken: The American Iconoclast,* pp. 141–144.

64. Ibid., p. 475.

65. Edmund Wilson, "Mencken's Democratic Man," *The New Republic,* December 15, 1926, p. 110.

66. Ibid.

67. Ibid., p. 111.

68. Ibid.

69. H. L. Mencken, *A Mencken Chrestomathy* (New York: Vintage Books, 1982), p. viii. *Chrestomathy* was first published in 1949 by Alfred A. Knopf. All references throughout this book are to the 1982 Vintage edition.

70. Ibid., p. vii.

71. Ibid., p. viii.

72. Charles A. Fecher, *Mencken: A Study of His Thought*, p. 219.

73. Conor Brady, "Warrior Armed With Words," *Irish Times*, April 8, 2006. This seems to be not only the recent prevailing point of view of the European press (Britain, Ireland, Scotland, Germany, Norway) but also of many American publications, including those of conservative bent.

74. H. L. Mencken, "The Library," the *American Mercury*, April 1928, p. 510.

Editorial Note

The first limited edition of *Notes on Democracy* was published in 1926 by Alfred A. Knopf and consisted of 235 copies, signed by the author. Thirty-five copies were printed on Japan Vellum, of which five were not for sale, and two hundred on Borzoi rag paper, of which eight were not for sale. The first trade edition was published on October 20, 1926. A second edition was released in November 1926. The English edition was published in February 1927 by Jonathan Cape (London). A German translation, *Demokratenspiegel*, was issued in Berlin by Widerstands Verlag in 1930, and was translated by Dora Sophie Kellner.* In 1977, Octagon Books, a division of Farrar, Straus & Giroux, published a reprint of *Notes on Democracy* through a special arrangement with Knopf, Inc.

Annotations have been provided to identify names, places, and events and to clarify otherwise obscure allusions. They are not aimed at the expert but at a younger generation. Ned Conquest, Jean-Marc Jezequel, and Bianca Schroder provided translations respectively for the Latin, French, and German words and phrases.

*Richard J. Schrader, with the assistance of George H. Thompson and Jack R. Sanders, *H. L. Mencken: A Descriptive Bibliography* (Pittsburgh: University of Pittsburgh Press, 1998), pp. 165–171; Betty Adler, with the assistance of Jane Wilhelm, *H.L.M.: The Mencken Bibliography* (Baltimore: The Johns Hopkins Press, 1961), p. 12.

I
Democratic Man

1.
His Appearance in the World

DEMOCRACY CAME INTO THE WESTERN WORLD TO THE TUNE of sweet, soft music. There was, at the start, no harsh bawling from below; there was only a dulcet twittering from above. Democratic man thus began as an ideal being, full of ineffable virtues and romantic wrongs—in brief, as Rousseau's noble savage[1] in smock and jerkin, brought out of the tropical wilds to shame the lords and masters of the civilized lands. The fact continues to have important consequences to this day. It remains impossible, as it was in the Eighteenth Century, to separate the democratic idea from the theory that there is a mystical merit, an esoteric and ineradicable rectitude, in the man at the bottom of the scale—that inferiority, by some strange magic, becomes a sort of superiority—nay, the superiority of superiorities. Everywhere on earth, save where the enlightenment of the modern age is confessedly in transient eclipse, the movement is toward the completer and more enamoured enfranchisement of the lower orders. Down there, one hears, lies a deep, illimitable reservoir of righteousness and wisdom, unpolluted by the corruption of privilege. What baffles statesmen is to be solved by the people, instantly and by a sort of seraphic intuition. Their yearnings are pure; they alone are capable of a perfect patriotism; in them is the only hope of peace and happiness on this lugubrious ball. The cure for the evils of democracy is more democracy!

This notion, as I hint, originated in the poetic fancy of gentlemen on the upper levels—sentimentalists who, observing to their distress that the ass was over-laden, proposed to reform transport by putting him into the cart. A stale Christian bilge ran through their veins, though many of them, as it happened, toyed with what is now called Modernism.[2] They were the direct ancestors of the more saccharine Liberals[3] of to-day, who yet mouth their tattered phrases and dream their preposterous dreams. I can find no record that these phrases, in the beginning, made much impression upon the actual objects of their rhetoric. Early democratic man seems to have given little thought to the democratic ideal, and less veneration. What he wanted was something concrete and highly materialistic—more to eat, less work, higher wages, lower taxes. He had no apparent belief in the acroamatic[4] virtue of his own class, and certainly none in its capacity to rule. His aim was not to exterminate the baron, but simply to bring the baron back to a proper discharge of baronial business. When, by the wild shooting that naturally accompanies all mob movements, the former end was accidentally accomplished, and men out of the mob began to take on baronial airs, the mob itself quickly showed its opinion of them by butchering them deliberately and in earnest. Once the pikes were out, indeed, it was a great deal more dangerous to be a tribune of the people than to be an ornament of the old order. The more copiously the blood gushed, the nearer that old order came to resurrection. The Paris proletariat, having been misled into killing its King in 1793, devoted the next two years to killing those who had misled it, and by the middle of 1796 it had another King in fact, and in three years more he was King *de jure*,[5] with an attendant herd of barons, counts, marquises and dukes, some of them new but most of them old, to guard, symbolize and execute his sovereignty. And he and they were immensely popular—so popular that half France leaped to suicide that their glory might blind the world.

Meanwhile, of course, there had been a certain seeping down of democratic theory from the metaphysicians to the mob—obscured by the uproar, hut still going on. Rhetoric, like a stealthy plague, was doing its immemorial work. Where men were confronted by the harsh, exigent realities of battle and pillage, as they were everywhere on the Continent, it got into their veins only slowly, but where they had time to listen to oratory, as in England and, above all, in America, it fetched them more quickly. Eventually, as the world grew exhausted and the wars passed, it began to make its effects felt everywhere. Democratic man, contemplating himself, was suddenly warmed by the spectacle. His condition had plainly improved. Once a slave, he was now only a serf. Once condemned to silence, he was now free to criticize his masters, and even to flout them, and the ordinances of God with them. As he gained skill and fluency at that sombre and fascinating art, he began to heave in wonder at his own merit. He was not only, it appeared, free to praise and damn, challenge and remonstrate; he was also gifted with a peculiar rectitude of thought and will, and a high talent for ideas, particularly on the political plane. So his wishes, in his mind, began to take on the dignity of legal rights, and after a while, of intrinsic and natural rights, and by the same token the wishes of his masters sank to the level of mere ignominious lusts. By 1828 in America and by 1848 in Europe[6] the doctrine had arisen that all moral excellence, and with it all pure and unfettered sagacity, resided in the inferior four-fifths of mankind. In 1867 a philosopher out of the gutter pushed that doctrine to its logical conclusion.[7] He taught that the superior minority had no virtues at all, and hence no rights at all—that the world belonged exclusively and absolutely to those who hewed its wood and drew its water. In less than half a century he had more followers in the world, open and covert, than any other sophist since the age of the Apostles.

Since then, to be sure, there has been a considerable recession from that extreme position. The dictatorship of the proletariat, tried here and there, has turned out to be—if I may venture a prejudiced judgment—somewhat impracticable. Even the most advanced Liberals, observing the thing in being, have been moved to cough sadly behind their hands. But it would certainly be going beyond the facts to say that the underlying democratic dogma has been abandoned, or even appreciably overhauled. To the contrary, it is now more prosperous than ever before. The late war[8] was fought in its name, and it was embraced with loud hosannas by all the defeated nations. Everywhere in Christendom it is now official, save in a few benighted lands where God is temporarily asleep. Everywhere its fundamental axioms are accepted: *(a)* that the great masses of men have an inalienable right, born of the very nature of things, to govern themselves, and *(b)* that they are competent to do it. Are they occasionally detected in gross and lamentable imbecilities? Then it is only because they are misinformed by those who would exploit them: the remedy is more education. Are they, at times, seen to be a trifle naughty, even swinish? Then it is only a natural reaction against the oppressions they suffer: the remedy is to deliver them. The central aim of all the Christian governments of to-day, in theory if not in fact, is to further their liberation, to augment their power, to drive ever larger and larger pipes into the great reservoir of their natural wisdom. That government is called good which responds most quickly and accurately to their desires and ideas. That is called bad which conditions their omnipotence and puts a question mark after their omniscience.

2.
Varieties of Homo Sapiens

So much for the theory. It seems to me, and I shall here contend, that all the known facts lie flatly against it—that there is actually no more evidence for the wisdom of the inferior man, nor for his virtue, than there is for the notion that Friday is an unlucky day. There was, perhaps, some excuse for believing in these phantasms in the days when they were first heard of in the world, for it was then difficult to put them to the test, and what cannot be tried and disproved has always had a lascivious lure for illogical man. But now we know a great deal more about the content and character of the human mind than we used to know, both on high levels and on low levels, and what we have learned has pretty well disposed of the old belief in its congenital intuitions and inherent benevolences. It is, we discover, a function, at least mainly, of purely physical and chemical phenomena, and its development and operation are subject to precisely the same natural laws which govern the development and operation, say, of the human nose or lungs. There are minds which start out with a superior equipment, and proceed to high and arduous deeds; there are minds which never get any further than a sort of insensate sweating, like that of a kidney. We not only observe such differences; we also begin to chart them with more or less accuracy. Of one mind we may say with some confidence that it shows an extraordinary capacity for function and development—that its possessor, exposed to a suitable process of training, may be trusted to acquire the largest body of knowledge and the highest skill at ratiocination to which *Homo sapiens* is adapted. Of another we may say with the same confidence that its abilities are sharply limited—that no conceivable training can move it beyond a certain point. In other words, men differ inside their heads as they differ outside. There are men who are naturally intelligent and can learn, and there are men who are naturally stupid and cannot.

Here, of course, I flirt with the so-called intelligence tests,[1] and so bring down upon my head that acrid bile which they have set to flowing. My plea in avoidance is that I have surely done my share of damning them: they aroused, when they were first heard of, my most brutish passions, for pedagogues had them in hand. But I can only say that time and experience have won me to them, for the evidence in favor of them slowly piles up, pedagogues or no pedagogues. In other words, they actually work. What they teach is borne out by immense accumulations of empiric corroboration. It is safe, nine times out of ten, to give them credence, and so it seems to me to be safe to generalize from them. Is it only a coincidence that their most frantic critics are the Liberals, which is to say, the only surviving honest believers in democracy? I think not. These Liberals, whatever their defects otherwise, are themselves capable of learning, and so they quickly mastered the fact that MM. Simon and Binet[2] offered the most dangerous menace to their vapourings ever heard of since the collapse of the Holy Alliance.[3] Their dudgeon followed. In two ways the tests give aid and comfort to their enemies. First, they provide a more or less scientific means of demonstrating the difference in natural intelligence between man and man—a difference noted ages ago by common observation, and held to be real by all men save democrats, at all times and everywhere. Second, they provide a rational scale for measuring it and a rational explanation of it. Intelligence is reduced to levels, and so given a reasonable precision of meaning. An intelligent man is one who is capable of taking in knowledge until the natural limits of the species are reached. A stupid man is one whose progress is arrested at some specific time and place before then. There thus appears in psychology—and the next instant in politics—the concept of the unteachable. Some men can learn almost indefinitely; their capacity goes on increasing until their bodies begin to wear out. Others stop in childhood, even in infancy. They reach, say, the mental age of ten or twelve, and then they develop no more. Physically, they become men, and sprout beards, political delusions, and the desire to propagate their kind. But mentally they remain on the level of schoolboys.

The fact here is challenged sharply by the democrats aforesaid, but certainly not with evidence. Their objection to it is rather of a metaphysical character, and involves gratuitous, transcendental assumptions as to what ought and what ought not to be true. They echo also, of course, the caveats of other and less romantic critics, some of them very ingenious; but always, when hard pressed, they fall back pathetically upon the argument that believing such things would be in contempt of the dignity of man, made in God's image. Is this argument sound? Is it, indeed, new? I seem to have heard it long ago, from the gentlemen of the sacred faculty. Don't they defend the rubbish of Genesis on the theory that rejecting it would leave the rabble without faith, and that without faith it would be one with the brutes, and very unhappy, and, what is worse, immoral? I leave such contentions to the frequenters of Little Bethel,[4] and pause only to observe that if the progress of the human race had depended upon them we'd all believe in witches, ectoplasms and madstones to-day. Democracy, alas, is also a form of theology, and shows all the immemorial stigmata. Confronted by uncomfortable* facts, it invariably tries to dispose of them by appeals to the highest sentiments of the human heart. An anti-democrat is not merely mistaken; he is also wicked, and the more plausible he is the more wicked he becomes. As I have said, the earliest of modern democrats were full of Christian juices. Their successors never get very far from Genesis I, 27.[5] They are Fundamentalists[6] by instinct, however much they may pretend to a mellow scepticism.

One undoubted fact gives them a certain left-handed support, though they are far too discreet to make use of it. I allude to the fact that man on the lower levels, though he quickly reaches the limit of his capacity for taking in actual knowledge, remains capable for a long time thereafter of absorbing delusions. What is true daunts him, but what is *not* true finds lodgment in his cranium with so little resistance that there is only a trifling emission of

*Correcting "uncomfortabe" in original text.

heat. I shall go back to this singular and beautiful phenomenon later on. It lies at the heart of what is called religion, and at the heart of all democratic politics no less. The thinking of what Charles Richet[7] calls *Homo stultus*[8] is almost entirely in terms of palpable nonsense. He has a dreadful capacity for embracing and cherishing impostures. His history since the first records is a history of successive victimizations—by priests, by politicians, by all sorts and conditions of quacks. His heroes are always frauds. In all ages he has hated bitterly the men who were labouring most honestly and effectively for the progress of the race. What such men teach is beyond his grasp. He believes in consequence that it is unsound, immoral and of the devil.

3.
The New Psychology

The concept of arrested development has caused an upheaval in psychology, and reduced the arduous introspections of the old-time psychologists to a series of ingenious but unimportant fancies. Men are *not* alike, and very little can be learned about the mental processes of a congressman, an ice-wagon driver or a cinema actor by studying the mental processes of a genuinely superior man. The difference is not only qualitative; it is also, in important ways, quantitative. One thus sees the world as a vast field of greased poles, flying gaudy and seductive flags. Up each a human soul goes shinning, painfully and with many a slip. Some climb eventually to the high levels; a few scale the dizziest heights. But the great majority never get very far from the ground. There they struggle for a while, and then give it up. The effort is too much for them; it doesn't seem to be worth its agonies. Golf is easier; so is joining Rotary; so is Fundamentalism; so is osteopathy; so is Americanism.[1]

In an aristocratic society government is a function of those who have got relatively far up the poles, either by their own prowess or by starting from the shoulders of their fathers–which is to say, either by God's grace or by God's grace. In a democratic society it is the function of all, and hence mainly of those who have got only a few spans from the ground. Their eyes, to be sure, are still thrown toward the stars. They contemplate, now bitterly, now admiringly, the backsides of those who are above them. They are bitter when they sense anything rationally describable as actual superiority; they admire when what they see is fraud. Bitterness and admiration, interacting, form a complex of prejudices which tends to cast itself into more or less stable forms. Fresh delusions, of course, enter into it from time to time, usually on waves of frantic emotion, but it keeps its main outlines. This complex of prejudices is what is known, under democracy, as public opinion. It is the glory of democratic states.

Its content is best studied by a process of analysis—that is, by turning from the complex whole to the simpler parts. What does the mob think? It thinks, obviously, what its individual members think. And what is that? It is, in brief, what somewhat sharp-nosed and unpleasant children think. The mob, being composed, in the overwhelming main, of men and women who have not got beyond the ideas and emotions of childhood, hovers, in mental age, around the time of puberty, and chiefly below it. If we would get at its thoughts and feelings we must look for light to the thoughts and feelings of adolescents. The old-time introspective psychology[2] offered little help here. It concerned itself almost exclusively with the mental processes of the more reflective, and hence the superior sort of adults; it fell into the disastrous fallacy of viewing a child as simply a little man. Just as modern medicine, by rejecting a similar fallacy on the physical plane, has set up the science and art of pediatrics, so the new behaviourist psychology has given a new dignity and autonomy to the study of the child mind. The first steps were very difficult. The behaviourists[3] not only had to invent an entirely new technique, like the pediatricians before them; they also had to meet the furious opposition of the orthodox psychologists, whose moony speculations they laughed at and whose authority they derided. But they persisted, and the problems before them turned out, in the end, to be relatively simple, and by no means difficult to solve. By observing attentively what was before everyone's nose they quickly developed facts which left the orthodox psychologists in an untenable and absurd position. One by one, the old psychological categories went overboard, and with them a vast mass of vague and meaningless psychological terminology.

On the cleared ground remained a massive discovery: that the earliest and most profound of human emotions is fear. Man comes into the world weak and naked, and almost as devoid of intelligence as an oyster, but he brings with him a highly complex and sensitive susceptibility to fear. He can tremble and cry out in the first hours of his life—nay, in the first minute. Make a loud noise behind an infant just born, and it will shake like a Sunday-school superintendent taken in adultery. Take away its support—that is, make it believe that it is falling—and it will send up such a whoop as comes from yokels when the travelling tooth-puller has at them. These fears, by their character, suggest that they have a phylogenic origin—that is, that they represent inherited race experience, out of the deep darkness and abysm of time. Dr. John B. Watson,[4] the head of the behaviourist school, relates them to the daily hazards of arboreal man—the dangers presented by breaking tree branches. The ape-man learned to fear the sudden, calamitous plunge, and he learned to fear, too, the warning crack. One need not follow Dr. Watson so far; there is no proof, indeed, that man was ever arboreal. But it must be obvious that this emotion of fear is immensely deep-seated—that it is instinctive if anything is instinctive. And all the evidence indicates that every other emotion is subordinate to it. None other shows itself so soon, and none other enters so powerfully into the first functioning of the infant mind. And to the primeval and yet profoundly rational fears that it brings into the world it quickly adds others that depart farther and farther from rationality. It begins to fear ideas as well as things, strange men as well as hostile nature. It picks up dreads and trepidations from its mother, from its nurse, from other children. At the age of three years, as Dr. Watson shows, its mental baggage is often little more than a vast mass of such things. It has anxieties, horrors, even superstitions. And as it increases in years it adds constantly to the stock.

The process of education is largely a process of getting rid of such fears. It rehearses, after a fashion, the upward struggle of man. The ideal educated man is simply one who has put away as foolish the immemorial fears of the race—of strange men and strange ideas, of the powers and principalities of the air. He is sure of himself in the world; no dread of the dark rides him; he is serene. To produce such men is the central aim of every rational system of education; even under democracy it is one of the aims, though perhaps only a subordinate one. What brings it to futility is simply the fact that the vast majority of men are congenitally incapable of any such intellectual progress. They cannot take in new ideas, and they cannot get rid of old fears. They lack the logical sense; they are unable to reason from a set of facts before them, free from emotional distraction. But they also lack something more fundamental: they are incompetent to take in the bald facts themselves. Here I point to the observations of Dr. Eleanor R. Wembridge,[5] a practical psychologist of great shrewdness. Her contribution is the discovery that the lower orders of men, though they seem superficially to use articulate speech and thus to deal in ideas, are actually but little more accomplished in that way than so many trained animals. Words, save the most elemental, convey nothing to them. Their minds cannot grasp even the simplest abstractions; all their thinking is done on the level of a few primitive appetites and emotions. It is thus a sheer impossibility to educate them, as much so as it would be if they were devoid of the five senses. The schoolmarm who has at them wastes her time shouting up a rain-spout. They are imitative, as many of the lower animals are imitative, and so they sometimes deceive her into believing that her expositions and exhortations have gone home, but a scientific examination quickly reveals that they have taken in almost nothing. Thus ideas leave them unscathed; they are responsive only to emotions, and their emotions are all elemental—the emotions, indeed, of tabby-cats rather than of men.

4.
Politics Under Democracy

Fear remains the chiefest of them. The demagogues, *i.e.*, the professors of mob psychology, who flourish in democratic states are well aware of the fact, and make it the corner-stone of their exact and puissant science. Politics under democracy consists almost wholly of the discovery, chase and scotching of bugaboos. The statesman becomes, in the last analysis, a mere witch-hunter, a glorified smeller and snooper,[1] eternally chanting "Fe, Fi, Fo, Fum!" It has been so in the United States since the earliest days. The whole history of the country has been a history of melodramatic pursuits of horrendous monsters, most of them imaginary: the red-coats, the Hessians, the monocrats, again the red-coats, the Bank, the Catholics, Simon Legree, the Slave Power, Jeff Davis, Mormonism, Wall Street, the rum demon, John Bull, the hell hounds of plutocracy, the trusts, General Weyler, Pancho Villa, German spies, hyphenates, the

Kaiser, Bolshevism.[2] The list might be lengthened indefinitely; a complete chronicle of the Republic could be written in terms of it, and without omitting a single important episode. It was long ago observed that the plain people, under democracy, never vote *for* anything, but always *against* something. The fact explains, in large measure, the tendency of democratic states to pass over statesmen of genuine imagination and sound ability in favour of colourless mediocrities. The former are shining marks, and so it is easy for demagogues to bring them down; the latter are preferred because it is impossible to fear them. The demagogue himself, when he grows ambitious and tries to posture as a statesman, usually comes ignominiously to grief, as the cases of Bryan, Roosevelt and Wilson[3] dramatically demonstrate. If Bryan had confined* himself, in 1896, to the chase of the bugaboo of plutocracy, it is very probable that he would have been elected. But he committed the incredible folly of throwing most of his energies into advocating a so-called constructive program,[4] and it was thus easy for his opponents to alarm the mob against him. That program had the capital defect of being highly technical, and hence almost wholly unintelligible to all save a small minority; so it took on a sinister look, and caused a shiver to go down the democratic spine. It was his cross-of-gold speech[5] that nominated him; it was his cow State political economy that ruined him. Bryan was a highly unintelligent man, a true son of the mob, and thus never learned anything by experience. In his last days he discovered a new issue in the evolutionary hypothesis.[6] It was beyond the comprehension of the mob, and hence well adapted to arousing its fears. But he allowed his foes[7] to take the offensive out of his hands, and in the last scene of all he himself was the pursued, and the tide of the battle was running so heavily against him that even the hinds at Dayton, Tenn., were laughing at him.

*Correcting "comfined" in original text.

Government under democracy is thus government by orgy, almost by orgasm. Its processes are most beautifully displayed at times when they stand most naked—for example, in war days. The history of the American share in the World War is simply a record of conflicting fears, more than once amounting to frenzies. The mob, at the start of the uproar, showed a classical reaction: it was eager only to keep out of danger. The most popular song, in the United States, in 1915,[8] was "I Didn't Raise My Boy to be a Soldier." In 1916, on his fraudulent promise to preserve that boy from harm, Wilson was reëlected. There then followed some difficult manœuvres—but perhaps not so difficult, after all, to skilful demagogues. The problem was to substitute a new and worse fear for the one that prevailed—a new fear so powerful that it would reconcile the mob to the thought of entering the war. The business was undertaken resolutely on the morning after election day. Thereafter, for three months, every official agency lent a hand. No ship went down[9] to a submarine's torpedo anywhere on the seven seas that the State Department did not report that American citizens—nay, American infants in their mothers' arms—were aboard. Diplomatic note followed diplomatic note, each new one surpassing all its predecessors in moral indignation. The Department of Justice ascribed all fires, floods and industrial accidents to German agents. The newspapers were filled with dreadful surmises, many of them officially inspired, about the probable effects upon the United States of the prospective German victory. It was obvious to everyone, even to the mob, that a victorious Germany would unquestionably demand an accounting for the United States' gross violations of neutrality. Thus a choice of fears was set up. The first was a fear of a Germany heavily beset, but making alarming progress against her foes. The second was a fear of a Germany delivered from them, and thirsting for revenge on a false and venal friend. The second fear soon engulfed the first. By the time February came the mob was reconciled to entering the war—reconciled, but surely not eager.

There remained the problem of converting reluctant acquiescence into enthusiasm. It was solved, as always, by manufacturing new fears. The history of the process remains to be written by competent hands: it will be a contribution to the literature of mob psychology of the highest importance. But the main outlines are familiar enough. The whole power of the government was concentrated upon throwing the plain people into a panic. All sense was heaved overboard, and there ensued a chase of bugaboos on a truly epic scale. Nothing like it had ever been seen in the world before, for no democratic state as populous as the United States had ever gone to war before. I pass over the details, and pause only to recall the fact that the American people, by the end of 1917, were in such terror that they lived in what was substantially a state of siege, though the foe was 3000 miles away and obviously unable to do them any damage. It was only the draft, I believe, that gave them sufficient courage to attempt actual hostilities. That ingenious device, by relieving the overwhelming majority of them of any obligation to take up arms, made them bold. Before it was adopted they were heavily in favour of contributing only munitions and money to the cause of democracy, with perhaps a few divisions of Regulars added for the moral effect. But once it became apparent that a given individual, John Doe, would not have to serve, he, John Doe, developed an altruistic eagerness for a frontal attack in force. For every Richard Roe in the conscript camps there were a dozen John Does thus safely at home, with wages high and the show growing enjoyable. So an heroic mood came upon the people, and their fear was concealed by a truculent front. But not from students of mob psychology.

5.
The Rôle of the Hormones

Two other emotions are observed in the raw human being, fresh from God's hands: one is rage, and the other is what, for want of a more accurate name, may be called love. This love, of course, is something quite different from the thing that poets sing. It is a great deal more earthly, and perhaps a great deal more honest. It manifests itself typically in a delight in being tickled; its psychic overtones take the form of being amiable. The child that is capable of it in the fullest measure is the one that coos loudest when its mother pats and strokes it, and tucks it into bed. In these sad days, when every flapper has read Freud[1] and ponders on the libido, there is no need, I take it, for me to explain that such delights have their seats chiefly in erogenous zones, and have more to do with the hormones than with the soul. Here the new child psychology confirms the observations of the Freudians, and reinforces their allegation that even the most tender and innocent infant may be worthy of suspicion. Dr. Watson says that the dreadful phenomenon of tumescence in the male can occur at birth—a satirical fact of the first calibre, if a fact. It concerns us here only because the incurable infantilism of the inferior man brings him to manhood with his emotions in this department substantially what they were when he yielded himself to auto-erotic exercises in the cradle.

But there is yet a difference, and it is important. In character his amorous fancies are the same; in intensity they are immensely exaggerated. His brain, in the first years of his second decade, ceases to develop, but simultaneously his glands begin to unfold gloriously, and presently they dominate his whole organism. In his middle teens, he is no more than a vast geyser of hormones. The sweet passion of love, in these years, is to him precisely what it is to a Tom cat. If he is of the bucolic variety of *Homo stultus* he has his will of his neighbour's daughter, and there begins a race between the village pastor and the village *sage-femme.*[2] If he is of the urban proletariat, he finds the outer world more inhospitable to the inner urge, for there are no dark lanes in the cities and no moonlight nights, but the urge itself remains irresistible and so in some way or other, vicariously or in harsh physiological terms, he yields himself to it, and loses his immortal soul.

Later on the thing grows more subtle and even more refined. His vast capacity for illusion, his powerful thirst for the not true, embellishes his anthropoid appetite without diminishing it, and he begins to toy with sentiment, even with a sort of poetry. If you want to discover the content of that poetry go look at any movie, or listen to any popular song. At its loftiest, it is never far from the poetry of a rooster in a barnyard. Love, to the inferior man, remains almost wholly a physical matter. The heroine he most admires is the one who offers the grossest sexual provocation; the hero who makes his wife roll her eyes is a perambulating phallus. The eminent psychologists who conduct tabloid newspapers make this fact the corner-stone of their metaphysical system. Their ideal piece of news is one in which nothing is left to the imagination that can be wormed through the mails.[3] Their readers want no sublimation and no symbolism.

Love, as Freud explains, has many meanings. It runs from the erotic to the philanthropic. But in all departments and on all planes the inferior man reduces it to terms of his own elemental yearnings. Of all his stupidities there is none more stupid than that which makes it impossible for him to see beyond them, even as an act of the imagination. He simply cannot formulate the concept of a good that is not his own good. The fact explains his immemorial heat against heretics, sacred and secular. His first thought and his last thought, contemplating them, is to stand them up against a wall, and have at them with musketry. Go back into history as far as you please, and you will find no record that he has ever opened his mouth for fairness, for justice, for decency between man and man. Such concepts, like the concepts of honour and of liberty, are eternally beyond him, and belong only to his superiors. The slaughters in the Roman arena delighted him; he applauded Torquemada;[4] only yesterday he was marching against radicals—*i.e.*, idiots who lamented his exploitation and sought to end it—with the American Legion.[5] His natural cowardice, of course, moves him powerfully in such situations: his congenital fear is easily translated into cruelty. But something must also be said for his mere incapacity to project himself into the place of the other, his deficiency in imagination. Are the poor charitable? Then it is only to the poor. When their betters stand before them, asking for something that they may withhold—when they are thus confronted, though the thing asked for be only fair dealing, elemental justice, common decency, they are wolves.

In a previous work I have adverted to the appalling development of this wolfishness among peasants.[6] They may be safely assumed, I believe, to represent the lowest caste among civilized men. They are the closest, both in their avocations and in their mental processes, to primeval man. One may think of them as the sediment remaining in the filter after the stream of progress has gone through. Even the city proletariat is appreciably superior, if only because it embraces those more intelligent yokels who have had the wit to escape from the dreadful drudgery of the dunghill. Well, give a glance at the theology and politics prevailing on the land. The former, in all countries and all ages, has kept contact with the primitive animism of savages: it bristles everywhere with demons, witches and ghosts. In its public aspect it is as intolerant of heresy as Thibetan lamaism. The yokel not only believes that all heretics are doomed to be roasted in hell through all eternity; he also holds that they should be harassed as much as possible on this earth. The anti-evolution laws of the South afford an instructive glimpse into the peasant mind. They are based frankly upon the theory that every man who dissents from the barnyard theology is a scoundrel, and devoid of civil rights. That theory was put very plainly by the peasant attorney-general[7] during the celebrated Scopes trial, to the visible satisfaction of the peasant judge.

In politics the virtuous clod-hopper, again speaking for inferior man, voices notions of precisely the same sort. The whole process of government, as he views it, is simply a process of promoting his private advantage. He can imagine no good save his own good. When his affairs are prospering—which is to say, when the needs of the city man are acute, and the latter is thus at his mercy—he rams his advantage home with relentless ferocity. For him to show any altruism in such a situation, or even any common humanity, would be so strange as to appear fabulous. But when things are running against him he believes that the city man should be taxed to make up his losses: this is the alpha and omega of all the brummagem progressivism that emanates from the farm.[8] That "progressivism," in the hands of political mountebanks, is swathed in the trappings of Service,[9] but at the heart of it there is nothing but bald self-seeking. The yokel hates everyone who is not a yokel—and is afraid of everyone. He is democratic man in the altogether. He is the glory and bulwark of all democratic states. The city proletarian may be flustered and run amok by ideas—ideas without any sense, true enough, but still ideas. The yokel has room in his head for only one. That is the idea that God regards him fondly, and has a high respect for him—that all other men are out of favour in heaven and abandoned to the devil.

6.
Envy As a Philosophy

But under this pretension to superiority, of course, there lies an uncomfortable realization of actual inferiority. The peasant hates; *ergo,* he envies—and "'l'envie," as Heine said to Philarète Chasles, "est une infériorité qui s'avoue."[1] The disdain that goes with genuine superiority is something quite different; there is no sign of it in him. He is so far from it, indeed, that he can imagine no higher delights than such as proceed from acts which, when performed by the hated city man, he denounces as crimes, and tries to put down by law. It is the cabaret that makes a Prohibitionist of him, not the drunkard in the gutter. Doomed himself to drink only crude and unpalatable stimulants, incompetently made and productive of depressing malaises, and forced to get them down in solitary swinishness behind the door, he naturally longs for the varieties that have a more delicate and romantic smack, and are ingested in gay society and to the music of harps and sackbuts. That longing is vain. There are no cabarets in the village, but only sordid speakeasies, selling raw spirits out of filthy jugs. Drinking cider in the barn is so lonely as to be a sort of onanism. Where is the music? Where are the whirling spangles, the brilliant lights? Where is the swooning, suffocating scent of lilies-of-the-valley, Jockey Club?[2] Where, above all, are the lost and fascinating females, so thrillingly described by the visiting evangelist? The yokel peeks through a crack in the barn-door and glimpses his slatternly wife laboriously rounding up strayed pigs: to ask her in for a friendly bumper[3] would be as appalling as asking in the cow. So he gets down his unappetizing dram, feels along his glabella for the beginning headache, and resumes his melancholy heaving of manure—a Prohibitionist by conscience, doubly-riveted and immovable.

In all his politics this envy is manifest. He hates the plutocrats of the cities, not only because they best him in the struggle for money, but also because they spend their gains in debaucheries that are beyond him. Such yellow-backs as "Night Life in Chicago"[4] have done more, I believe, to propagate "idealism" in the corn-and-hog belt than all the eloquence of the Pfeffers and Bryans.[5] The yokels, reading them in secret, leave them full of a passionate conviction that such Babylonish revels must be put down, if Christianity is to survive—that it is obviously against the will of God that a Chicago stockbroker should have five wives and fifty concubines, and an Iowa swineherd but one—and that one a strictly Christian woman, even at the purple moments when wits and principles tend naturally to scatter. In the cities, as everyone knows, women move toward antinomianism: it is a scandal throughout Christendom. Their souls, I daresay, are imperilled thereby, but certainly no one argues that it makes them less charming—least of all the husbandman behind his remote plough, tortured by ruby reflections of the carnalities at Atlantic City and Miami. On the land, however, that movement has but little genuine force, despite a general apeing of its externals. The female young may bob their hair, but they do not reject divine revelation. I am told by experts that it is still a sort of marvel, as it was in the youth of Abraham Lincoln, to find a farm-wife who has definitely renounced the theology of the local pastors. The fact has obvious moral—and, by an easy step, political—consequences. There are about six and a half million farmers in the United States. Keep in mind the fact that at least six millions of them are forced to live in unmitigated monogamy with wives whose dominant yearning is to save the heathen hordes in India from hell fire, and you will begin to get some grasp of the motives behind such statutes as the celebrated Mann Act.[6] The sea-sick passenger on the ocean liner detests the "good sailor" who stalks past him a hundred times a day, obscenely smoking large, greasy, gold-banded cigars. In precisely the same way democratic man hates the fellow who is having a better time of it in this world. Such, indeed, is the origin of democracy. And such is the origin of its twin, Puritanism.

The city proletarian, of course, is a cut above the hind, if only because his natural envy of his betters is mitigated and mellowed by *panem et circenses.*[7] His life may be swinish, but it is seldom dull. In good times there is actual money in his hand, and immense and complicated organizations offer him gaudy entertainment in return for it. In bad times his basic wants are met out of the community funds, and he is even kept in certain luxuries, necessary to his contentment. The immense development of public charity in the cities of the United States has yet to find adequate analysis and record. Nothing quite like it was ever known in past ages, nor is it paralleled in any other country to-day. What lies under it, I daresay, is simply the fact that the plutocracy of the Republic, having had more experience with democracy than the plutocracy anywhere else, has attained to a higher skill in dealing with the proletarian. He is never dangerous so long as his belly is filled and his eyes kept a-pop; and in this great land, by Divine Providence, there is always enough surplus wealth, even in the worst times, to finance that filling and popping. The plethora of means has bred a large class of experts, professionally devoted to the business. They swarm in all the American cities, and when genuine wants fail them they invent artificial wants. This enterprise in the third theological virtue[8] has gone to great lengths. The proletarian, in his office as father, is now reduced by it to the simple biological function of a boar in a barn-yard. From the moment the fertilized ovum attaches itself to the *decidua serotina*[9] he is free to give himself whole-heartedly to politics, drink and the radio. There is elaborate machinery for instructing the partner of his ecstasies in the whole art and mystery of maternity, and all the accompanying expenses are provided for. Obstetricians of the highest eminence stand ready to examine her and counsel her; gynecologists are at hand to perform any necessary operations; trained nurses call at her home, supply and prepare her diet, warn her against a too animated social life, hand her instructive literature, and entertain her with anecdotes suitable to her condition. If she is too clumsy or too lazy to fashion a layette, or can't afford the materials, it is provided free of charge. And when she comes to term at last she is taken into a steam-heated hospital, boarded without cost, and delivered in a brilliant, aseptic, and, in so far as money can make it so, painless manner.

Nor is this all. Once she bas become a mother her benefits only increase. If she wants to get rid of her child it is taken off her hands, and eager propagandists instruct her in the science of avoiding another. If she chooses to keep it there is elaborate machinery for reducing the care and cost of it to nothing. Visiting nurses of a dozen different varieties stand ready to assume the burdens of washing it, dosing it with purges, and measuring out its victuals. Milk is supplied free—and not simply common cow's milk, but cow's milk modified according to the subtlest formulæ of eminent pediatricians. Ice is thrown in as a matter of course. Medicines are free at the neighbourhood dispensary. If the mother, recovering her figure, wishes to go shopping, she may park her baby at a *crèche*, and, on the plea that she is employed as a charwoman, leave it there all day. Once it can toddle the kindergarten yawns for it, and in holiday time the public playground, each officered by learned experts. The public school follows, and with it a host of new benefits. Dentists are in attendance to plug and pull the youngster's teeth at the public charge. Oculists fit it with horn-rimmed spectacles. It is deloused. Free lunches sustain it. Its books cost nothing. It is taught not only the three R's, but also raffia-work, bookkeeping, basketball, salesmanship, the new dances, and parliamentary law. It learns the causes of the late war and the fallacies of Socialism.

The rest you know as well as I do. The proletarian is so artfully relieved of the elemental gnawings which constantly terrorize the peasant and so steadily distracted from all sober thinking that his natural envy of his betters is sublimated into a sort of boozy contentment, like that of a hog in a comfortable sty. He escapes boredom, and with it, brooding. The political imbecilities which pile up in great waves from the prairies break upon the hard rock of his urban cynicism like rollers upon the strand. His pastors have but a slight hold upon him, and so cannot stir him up to the frantic hatreds which move the yokel. Even his wife emancipates herself from the ancient demonology of the race: his typical complaint against her is not that she is made anaphrodisiacal by Christian endeavour but that she is too worldly and extravagant, and spreads her charms too boldly. The rustic, alone upon his dung-hill, has time to nurse his grievances; the city moron is diverted from them by the shows that surround him. There was a time when yellow journalism[10] promised to prod him to dudgeon, and even to send him yelling to the barricades. But the plutocracy has deftly drawn its fangs, and in its place are the harmless tabloids. They ease his envy by giving him a vicarious share in the debaucheries of his economic superiors. He is himself, of course, unable to roar about the country in a high-powered car, accompanied by a beautiful coloured girl of large gifts for the art of love, but when he reads of the scions of old Knickerbocker[11] families doing it he somehow gets a touch of the thrill. It flatters him to think that he lives in a community in which such levantine joys are rife. Thus his envy is obscured by civic pride, by connoisseurship, and by a simple animal delight in good shows. By the time the tale reaches the yokel it is reduced to its immoral elements, and so makes him smell brimstone. But the city proletarian hears the froufrou of perfumed skirts.

7.
Liberty and Democratic Man

Under the festive surface, of course, envy remains: the proletarian is still a democrat. The fact shows itself grimly whenever the supply of *panem et circenses*[1] falls off sharply, and the harsh realities make themselves felt. All the revolutions in history have been started by hungry city mobs. The fact is, indeed, so plain that it has attracted the notice even of historians, and some of them deduce from it the doctrine that city life breeds a love of liberty. It may be so, but certainly that love is not visible in the lower orders. I can think of no city revolution that actually had liberty for its object, in any rational sense. The ideas of freedom that prevail in the world to-day were first formulated by country gentlemen, aided and abetted by poets and philosophers, with occasional help from an eccentric king. One of the most valid of them—that of free speech—was actually given its first support in law by the most absolute monarch of modern times, to wit, Frederick the Great.[2] When the city mob fights it is not for liberty, but for ham and cabbage. When it wins, its first act is to destroy every form of freedom that is not directed wholly to that end. And its second is to butcher all professional libertarians. If Thomas Jefferson had been living in Paris in 1793 he would have made an even narrower escape from the guillotine than Thomas Paine made.[3]

The fact is that liberty, in any true sense, is a concept that lies quite beyond the reach of the inferior man's mind. He can imagine and even esteem, in his way, certain false forms of liberty—for example, the right to choose between two political mountebanks, and to yell for the more obviously dishonest—but the reality is incomprehensible to him. And no wonder, for genuine liberty demands of its votaries a quality he lacks completely, and that is courage. The man who loves it must be willing to fight for it; blood, said Jefferson, is its natural manure.[4] More, he must be able to *endure* it—an even more arduous business. Liberty means self-reliance, it means resolution, it means enterprise, it means the capacity for doing without. The free man is one who has won a small and precarious territory from the great mob of his inferiors, and is prepared and ready to defend it and make it support him. All around him are enemies, and where he stands there is no friend. He can hope for little help from other men of his own kind, for they have battles of their own to fight. He has made of himself a sort of god in his little world, and he must face the responsibilities of a god, and the dreadful loneliness. Has *Homo boobiens*[5] any talent for this magnificent self-reliance? He has the same talent for it that he has for writing symphonies in the manner of Ludwig van Beethoven,[6] no less and no more. That is to say, he has no talent whatsoever, nor even any understanding that such a talent exists. Liberty is unfathomable to him. He can no more comprehend it than he can comprehend honour.[7] What he mistakes for it, nine times out of ten, is simply the banal right to empty hallelujahs upon his oppressors. He is an ox whose last proud, defiant gesture is to lick the butcher behind the ear.

"The vast majority of persons of our race," said Sir Francis Galton,[8] "have a natural tendency to shrink from the responsibility of standing and acting alone." It is a pity that the great pioneer of studies in heredity did not go beyond the fact to its obvious causes: they were exactly in his line. What ails "the vast majority of persons of our race" is simply the fact that, to their kind, even such mild and narrow liberties as they can appreciate are very recent acquisitions. It is barely a century and a half—a scant five generations—since four-fifths of the people of the world, white and black alike, were slaves, in reality if not in name. I could fill this book with evidence, indubitable and overwhelming. There are whole libraries upon the subject. Turn to any treatise on the causes of the French Revolution, and you will find the French peasant of 1780 but little removed, in legal rights and daily tasks, from the *fellahin* who built Cheops' pyramid. Consult any work on the rise of the Industrial System in England, and you will find the towns of that great liberty-loving land filled, in the same year, with a half-starved and anthropoid proletariat, and the countryside swarming with a dispossessed and despairing peasantry. Open any school-book of American history, and you will see Germans sold like cattle by their masters. If you thirst for more, keep on: the tale was precisely the same in Italy, in Spain, in Russia, in Scandinavia, and in what remained of the Holy Roman Empire. The Irish, at the close of the Eighteenth Century, were clamped under a yoke that it took more than a century of effort to throw off. The Scotch, roving their bare intolerable hills, were only two steps removed from savagery, and even cannibalism. The Welsh, but recently delivered from voodooism to Methodism, were being driven into their own coal-mines. There was no liberty anywhere in Europe, even in name, until 1789, and there was little in fact until 1848. And in America? Again I summon the historians, some of whom begin to grow honest. America was settled largely by slaves, some escaped but others transported in bondage. The Revolution was imposed upon them by their betters, chiefly, in New England, commercial gents in search of greater profits, and in the South, country gentlemen ambitious to found a nobility in the wilderness. Universal manhood suffrage, the corner-stone of modern free states, was only dreamed of until 1867,[9] and economic freedom was little more than a name until years later.

Thus the lower orders of men, however grandiloquently they may talk of liberty to-day, have actually had but a short and highly deceptive experience of it. It is not in their blood. The grandfathers of at least half of them were slaves, and the great-grandfathers of three-fourths, and the great-great-grandfathers of seven-eighths, and the great-great-great-grandfathers of practically all. The heritage of freedom belongs to a small minority of men, descended, whether legitimately or by adultery, from the old lords of the soil or from the patricians of the free towns. It is my contention that such a heritage is necessary in order that the concept of liberty, with all its disturbing and unnatural implications, may be so much as grasped—that such ideas cannot be implanted in the mind of man at will, but must be bred in as all other basic ideas are bred in. The proletarian may mouth the phrases, as he did in Jefferson's day, but he cannot take in the underlying realities, as was also demonstrated in Jefferson's day. What his great-great-grandchildren may be capable of I am not concerned with here; my business is with the man himself as he now walks the world. Viewed thus, it must be obvious that he is still incapable of bearing the pangs of liberty. They make him uncomfortable; they alarm him; they fill him with a great loneliness. There is no high adventurousness in him, but only fear. He not only doesn't long for liberty; he is quite unable to stand it. What he longs for is something wholly different, to wit, security. He needs protection. He is afraid of getting hurt. All else is affectation, delusion, empty words.

The fact, as we shall see, explains many of the most puzzling political phenomena of so-called free states. The great masses of men, though theoretically free, are seen to submit supinely to oppression and exploitation of a hundred abhorrent sorts. Have they no means of resistance? Obviously they have. The worst tyrant, even under democratic plutocracy, has but one throat to slit. The moment the majority decided to overthrow him he would be overthrown. But the majority lacks the resolution; it cannot imagine taking the risk. So it looks for leaders with the necessary courage, and when they appear it follows them slavishly, even after their courage is discovered to be mere buncombe and their altruism only a cloak for more and worse oppressions. Thus it oscillates eternally between scoundrels, or, if you would take them at their own valuation, heroes. Politics becomes the trade of playing upon its natural poltroonery—of scaring it half to death, and then proposing to save it. There is in it no other quality of which a practical politician, taking one day with another, may be sure. Every theoretically free people wonders at the slavishness of all the others. But there is no actual difference between them.

8.
The Effects Upon Progress

It follows that the inferior man, being a natural slave himself, is quite unable to understand the desire for liberty in his superiors. If he apprehends that desire at all it is only as an appetite for a good of which he is himself incapable. He thus envies those who harbour it, and is eager to put them down. Justice, in fact, is always unpopular and in difficulties under democracy, save perhaps that false form of so-called social justice which is designed solely to get the laborer more than his fair hire. The wars of extermination that are waged against heretical minorities never meet with any opposition on the lower levels. The proletarian is always ready to help destroy the rights of his fellow proletarian, as was revealed brilliantly by the heroic services of the American Legion in the pogrom against Reds, just after the late war, and even more brilliantly by the aid that the American Federation of Labour[1] gave to the same gallant crusade. The city workman, oppressed by Prohibition, mourns the loss of his beer, not the loss of his liberty. He is ever willing to support similar raids upon the liberty of the other fellow, and he is not outraged when they are carried on in gross violation of the most elemental principles of justice and common decency. When, in a democratic state, any protest against such obscenities is heard at all, it comes from the higher levels. There a few genuine believers in liberty and justice survive, huddled upon a burning deck. It is to he marvelled at that most of them, on inspection, turn out to be the grandsons of similar heretics of earlier times? I think not. It takes quite as long to breed a libertarian as it takes to breed a race-horse. Neither may be expected to issue from a farm mare.

The whole progress of the world, even in the direction of ameliorating the lot of the masses, is always opposed by the masses. The notion that their clamour brought about all the governmental and social reforms of the last century, and that those reforms were delayed by the superior minority, is sheer nonsense; even Liberals begin to reject it as absurd. Consider, for example, the history of the American Department of Agriculture. Whatever the corruptions and imbecilities of this department in democratic hands, it must he plain to everyone that the net effect of its work over many years has been a series of immense benefits to the American farmer—benefits that have at once reduced his labour and augmented his profits. Nevertheless, it is a matter of history that the farmers of the United States, when the Department began as a bureau of the Patent Office in 1830, opposed it almost unanimously, and that for years their bitter derision kept it feeble. Without leaving the United States one may go even farther back. When John Adams, during his presidency, proposed to set up a Weather Bureau, he was denounced as an idiot and a scoundrel, as Henry Adams[2] has set forth in the introduction to "The Decay of Democratic Dogma." Examples from our own time are so numerous and notorious that it is needless to direct attention to them. It is axiomatic that all measures for safeguarding the public health are opposed by the majority, and that getting them upon the books is mainly a matter of deceiving and checkmating it. What happened in Los Angeles when a vaccination ordinance was submitted to a popular referendum is typical of what would happen anywhere under the same circumstances.[3] The ordinance was rejected, and smallpox spread in the town.* The proletariat, alarmed, then proceeded against it by going to Christian Scientists, osteopaths and chiropractors. Precisely the same thing happened in Switzerland.

Turn now to Germany, a country lately delivered from despotism by the arms of altruistic heroes. The social legislation of that country, for more than half a century, afforded a model to all other countries. All the workingmen's insurance, minimum wage, child labour and other such acts of the United States are bald imitations of it, and in England, before the war, the mountebank Lloyd-George[4] borrowed his whole bag of tricks from it. Well, Dr. Hans Delbrück,[5] in his "Regierung und Volkswille," tells† us that this legislation was fought step by step at home, and with the utmost ferocity, by the beneficiaries of it. When Bismarck[6] formulated it and essayed to get it through the Reichstag he was opposed by every mob-master in the Empire, save only his kept Socialist, Ferdinand Lassalle.[7] The common people were so heavily against him for several years that he had to carry on the government without the consent of the Reichstag—that is, unconstitutionally, and at the risk of his head. If the proletariat had been able to get control of the German courts, as it had got control of the Reichstag, it would have deposed him from office and condemned him to death for high treason. His treason consisted in trying to formulate a code of legislation designed to restore its old rights under the Prussian common law, destroyed by the rise of the industrial system, and to grant it many new and valuable benefits.

"Let any competently instructed person," says Sir Henry Maine,[8] "turn over in his mind the great epochs of scientific inven-

*Correcting the comma mark between "town" and "The" in original text.

†Correcting "tell" in original text.

tion and social change during the past two centuries, and consider what would have occurred if universal suffrage had been established at any one of them." Here, obviously, Sir Henry speaks of universal suffrage that is genuinely effective—suffrage that registers the actual will of the people accurately and automatically. As we shall see, no such thing exists in the world to-day, save in limited areas. Public policies are determined and laws are made by small minorities playing upon the fears and imbecilities of the mob—sometimes minorities of intelligent and honest men, but usually minorities of rogues. But the fact does not disturb the validity of Maine's argument. "Universal suffrage," he goes on, "would certainly have prohibited the spinning-jenny and the power loom. It would certainly have forbidden the threshing-machine. It would have prevented the adoption of the Gregorian Calender; it would have restored the Stuarts.[9] It would have proscribed the Roman Catholics, with the mob which burned Lord Mansfield's[10] house and library in 1780; and it would have proscribed the Dissenters, with the mob which burned Dr. Priestley's[11] house and library in 1791." So much for England. What of the United States? I point briefly to the anti-evolution acts which now begin to adorn the statute-books of the Hook-worm Belt, all of them supported vociferously by the lower orders. I point to the anti-vivisection and anti-contraception statutes,[12] to the laws licensing osteopaths and other such frauds, and to the multitude of acts depriving relatively enlightened minorities of the common rights of free assemblage and free speech. They increase in proportion as *vox populi*[13] is the actual voice of the state; they run with that "more democracy" which Liberals advocate. "Nothing in ancient alchemy," says Lecky,[14] "was more irrational than the notion that increased ignorance in the elective body will be converted into increased capacity for good government in the representative body; that the best way to improve the world and secure rational progress is to place government more and more under the control of the least enlightened classes."

The hostility of *Homo neandertalensis* to all exact knowledge, even when its effect is to work him benefits, is not hard to understand. He is against it because it is complex, and, to his dark mind, occult—because it puts an unbearable burden upon his meagre capacity for taking in ideas, and thus propels him into the realm of the unknowable and alarming. His search is always for short cuts, simple formulæ, revelation. All superstitions are such short cuts, whether they issue out of the African jungle or out of Little Bethel. So are all political platitudes and shibboleths. Their one aim is to make the unintelligible simple, and even obvious. No man who has not had a long and arduous education in the physical sciences can understand even the most elementary concepts of, say, pathology, but even a hind at the plow can take in the theory of chiropractic in two lessons. Hence the vast popularity of chiropractic among the submerged, and of osteopathy, Christian Science, spiritualism and all the other half rational and half supernatural quackeries with it. They are idiotic, like the tales displayed in the movies, but, again like the tales displayed in the movies, they are simple—and every man, high or low, prefers what he can understand to what puzzles and dismays him. The popularity of the farrago of absurdities called Fundamentalism—and it is popular among peasants, not only in the United States, but everywhere in Christendom—is thus easily understood. The cosmogonies that educated men toy with are all inordinately complex. To comprehend their veriest outlines requires an immense stock of exact knowledge and a special habit of thought, quite different in kind from the habit of thought which suffices for listening to the radio. It would be as vain to try to teach these cosmogonies to peasants as it would be to try to teach them to streptococci. But the cosmogony set forth in the first chapter of Genesis is so simple that a yokel can grasp it instantly. It collides ludicrously with many of the known facts, but he doesn't know the known facts. It is logically nonsensical, but to him the nonsensical, in the sciences as in politics, has an irresistible fascination. So he accepts the Word with loud hosannas, and has one more excuse for hating his betters.

Turn to any other field of knowledge, and the story remains the same. It is a tragic but inescapable fact that most of the finest fruits of human progress, like all of the nobler virtues of man, are the exclusive possession of small minorities, chiefly unpopular and disreputable. Of the sciences, as of the fine arts, the average human being, even in the most literate and civilized of modern States, is as ignorant as the horned cattle in the fields. What he knows of histology, say, or protozoölogy, or philology, or paleontology is precisely nothing. Such things lie beyond his capacity for learning, and he has no curiosity about them. The man who has any acquaintance with them seems to him to be a ridiculous figure, with a touch of the sinister. Even those applied sciences which enter intimately into his everyday existence remain outside his comprehension and interest. Consider, for example, chemistry and biology. The whole life of the inferior man, including especially his so-called thinking, is purely a biochemical process, and exactly comparable to what goes on in a barrel of cider, yet he knows no more about chemistry than a cow and no more about biology than its calf. The new physics, in the form of the radio, saves him from the appalling boredom of his hours of leisure, but physics itself remains as dark to him as theosophy. He is more ignorant of elementary anatomy and physiology than the Egyptian quacks of 4000 B.C. His knowledge of astronomy is confined to a few marvels, most of which he secretly doubts. He has never so much as heard of ethnology, pathology or embryology. Greek, to him, is only a jargon spoken by bootblacks, and Wagner[15] is a retired baseball player. He has never heard of Euripides, of Hippocrates, of Aristotle, or of Plato.[16] Or of Vesalius, Newton, and Roger Bacon.[17] The fine arts are complete blanks to him. He doesn't know what a Doric column is, or an etching, or a fugue. He is as ignorant of sonnets and the Gothic style as he is of ecclesiastical politics in Abyssinia.[18] Homer, Virgil, Cervantes, Bach, Raphael, Rubens, Beethoven[19] —all such colossal names are empty sounds to him, blowing idly down the wind. So far as he is concerned these great and noble men might as well have perished in the cradle. The stupendous beauties that they conjured into being are nothing to him: he sticks to the tabloids and the movies, with *Hot Dog*[20] or its like for Sunday afternoon. A politician by instinct and a statesman by divine right, he has never heard of "The Republic"[21] or "Leviathan."[22] A *Feinschmecker*[23] of pornography, he is unaware of Freud.

The Egyptian night[24] that hedges him round is not, perhaps, without its high uses and consolations. Learning survives among us largely because the mob has not got news of it. If the notions it turns loose descended to the lowest levels, there would be an uprising against them, and efforts would be made to put them down by law. In a previous treatise, adverting to this probability, I have sounded a warning against the fatuous effort to put the fine arts into the common-school curriculum in the United States. Its dangers are diminished, no doubt, by the fact that the teachers told off to execute it are themselves completely ignorant, but they remain dangers none the less. The peasants of Georgia, getting wind of the fact that grand operas were being played in Atlanta, demanded that the State Legislature discourage them with a tax of $1000 a performance. In the Middle West, after the late War, the American Legion proceeded with clubs against fiddlers who played Beethoven and Bach. Everywhere in America galleries of paintings are under suspicion, and in most States it is impossible for them to display works showing the female figure below the clavicle. Nor is this distrust of the fine arts confined to the rural sections. The most active censorship of literature, for example, is to be found in Boston. The Methodist anthropoids of the town, supported by the *Chandala*[25] of the Latin rite,[26] clerical and lay, carry on so violent a crusade against certain hated books, unquestionably of sound quality, that the local booksellers fear to stock them. Much of the best literature of the world, indeed, is forbidden to the Bostonian, heir though he may be to Emerson[27] and Thoreau.[28] If he would read it, he must procure it by stealth and read it behind the door, as a Kansan (imagining that so civilized a one exists) procures and consumes Clos Vougeot.[29]

In all this there is a great deal less of yearning for moral perfection than there is of mere hatred of beauty.[30] The common man, as a matter of fact, has no yearning for moral perfection. What ails him in that department is simply fear of punishment, which is to say, fear of his neighbours. He has, in safe privacy, the morals of a variety actor. Beauty fevers and enrages him for another and quite different reason. He cannot comprehend it, and yet it somehow challenges and disturbs him. If he could snore through good music he would not object to it; the trouble with it is that it keeps him awake. So he believes that it ought to be put down, just as he believes that political and economic ideas which disturb him and yet elude him ought to be put down. The finest art is safe from him simply because he has no contact with it, and is thus unaware of it. The fact, in this great Republic, saves the bacon of Johann Sebastian Bach. His music remains lawful because it lies outside the cognizance of the mob, and of the abandoned demagogues who make laws for the mob. It has thus something of the quality of the colours beyond violet and of the concept of honour. If by some abominable magic, it could be brought within range, it would at once arouse hostility. Its complexity would puzzle and dismay; its lack of utilitarian purpose[31] would affright. Soon there would be a movement to proscribe it, and Baptist clergymen would rove the land denouncing it, as they now denounce the plays of Shakespeare and the science of

Darwin. In the end some poor musician, taken playing it in rural Tennessee, would be hailed before a Judge Raulston, tried by a jury of morons, and railroaded to the calaboose.

9.
The Eternal Mob

Such is man on the nether levels. Such is the pet and glory of democratic states. Human progress passes him by. Its aims are unintelligible to him and its finest fruits are beyond his reach: what reaches him is what falls from the tree, and is shared with his four-footed brothers. He has changed but little since the earliest recorded time, and that change is for the worse quite as often as it is for the better. He still believes in ghosts, and has only shifted his belief in witches to the political sphere. He is still a slave to priests, and trembles before their preposterous magic. He is lazy, improvident and unclean. All the durable values of the world, though his labour has entered into them, have been created against his opposition. He can imagine nothing beautiful and he can grasp nothing true. Whenever he is confronted by a choice between two ideas, the one sound and the other not, he chooses almost infallibly, and by a sort of pathological compulsion, the one that is not. Behind all the great tyrants and butchers of history he has marched with loud hosannas, but his hand is eternally against those who seek to liberate the spirit of the race. He was in favour of Nero and Torquemada[1] by instinct, and he was against Galileo and Savonarola[2] by the same instinct. When a Cagliostro[3] dies he is ready for a Danton[4]; from the funeral of a Barnum[5] he rushes to the triumph of a Bryan. The world gets nothing from him save his brute labour, and even that he tries to evade. It owes nothing to him that has any solid dignity or worth, not even democracy. In two thousand years he has moved an inch: from the sports of the arena to the lynching-party—and another inch: from the obscenities of the Saturnalia[6] to the obscenities of the Methodist revival. So he lives out his life in the image of Jahveh.[7] What is worth knowing he doesn't know and doesn't want to know; what he knows is not true. The cardinal articles of his credo are the inventions of mountebanks; his heroes are mainly scoundrels.

Do I forget his central virtue—at least in Christendom? Do I forget his simple piety, his touching fidelity to the faith? I forget nothing: I simply answer, What faith? Is it argued by any rational man that the debased Christianity cherished by the mob in all the Christian countries of to-day has any colourable likeness to the body of ideas preached by Christ? If so, then let us have a better teaching of the Bible in the public-schools. The plain fact is that this bogus Christianity has no more relation to the system of Christ than it has to the system of Aristotle. It is the invention of Paul[8] and his attendant rabble-rousers—a body of men exactly comparable to the corps of evangelical pastors of to-day, which is to say, a body devoid of sense and lamentably indifferent to common honesty. The mob, having heard Christ, turned against Him, and applauded His crucifixion. His theological ideas were too logical and too plausible for it, and his ethical ideas were enormously too austere. What it yearned for was the old comfortable balderdash under a new and gaudy name, and that is precisely what Paul offered it. He borrowed from all the wandering dervishes and soul-snatchers of Asia Minor, and flavoured the stew with remnants of the Greek demonology. The result was a code of doctrines so discordant and so nonsensical that no two men since, examining it at length, have ever agreed upon its precise meaning. But Paul knew his mob: he had been a travelling labour leader. He knew that nonsense was its natural provender—that the unintelligible soothed it like sweet music. He was the *Stammvater*[9] of all the Christian mob-masters of to-day, terrorizing and enchanting the mob with their insane damnations, eating their seven fried chickens a week, passing the diligent plate, busy among the women. Once the early church emerged from the Roman catacombs and began to yield to that reorganization of society which was forced upon the ancient world by the barbarian invasions, Paul was thrown overboard as Methodists throw Wesley[10] overboard when they acquire the means and leisure for golf, and Peter[11] was put in his place. Peter was a blackguard, but he was at least free from any taint of Little Bethel. The Roman Church, in the aristocratic feudal age, promoted him *post mortem* to the Papacy, and then raised him to the mystical dignity of Rock,[12] a rank obviously quasi-celestial. But Paul remained the prophet of the sewers. He was to emerge centuries later in many incarnations—Luther,[13] Calvin,[14] Wesley, and so on. He remains to-day the arch-theologian of the mob. His turgid and witless metaphysics make Christianity bearable to men who would he repelled by Christ's simple and magnificent reduction of the duties of man to the duties of a gentleman.

II
The Democratic State

1.
The Two Kinds of Democracy

The lowly Christian I have limned is not only the glory of democratic states, but also their boss. Sovereignty is in him, sometimes both actually and legally, but always actually. Whatever he wants badly enough, he can get. If he is misled by mountebanks and swindled by scoundrels it is only because his credulity and imbecility cover a wider area than his simple desires. The precise form of the government he suffers under is of small importance. Whether it be called a constitutional monarchy, as in England, or a representative republic, as in France, or a pure democracy, as in some of the cantons of Switzerland, it is always essentially the same. There is, first, the mob, theoretically and in fact the ultimate judge of all ideas and the source of all power. There is, second, the camorra of self-seeking minorities, each seeking to inflame, delude and victimize it. The political process thus becomes a mere battle of rival rogues. But the mob remains quite free to decide between them. It may even, under the hand of God, decide for a minority that happens, by some miracle, to be relatively honest and enlightened. If, in common practice, it sticks to the thieves, it is only because their words are words it understands and their ideas are ideas it cherishes. It has the power to throw them off at will, and even at whim, and it also has the means.

A great deal of paper and ink has been wasted discussing the difference between representative government and direct democracy. The theme is a favourite one with university pundits, and also engages and enchants the stall-fed Rousseaus who arise intermittently in the cow States, and occasionally penetrate to Governors' mansions and the United States Senate. It is generally held that representative government, as practically encountered in the world, is full of defects, some of them amounting to organic disease. Not only does it take the initiative in lawmaking out of the hands of the plain people, and leave them only the function of referees; it also raises certain obvious obstacles to their free exercise of that function. Scattered as they are, and unorganized save in huge, unworkable groups, they are unable, it is argued, to formulate their virtuous desires quickly and clearly, or to bring to the resolution of vexed questions the full potency of their native sagacity. Worse, they find it difficult to enforce their decisions, even when they have decided. Every Liberal knows this sad story, and has shed tears telling it. The remedy he offers almost always consists of a resort to what he calls a purer democracy. That is to say, he proposes to set up the recall, the initiative and referendum, or something else of the sort, and so convert the representative into a mere clerk or messenger. The final determination of all important public questions, he argues, ought to be in the hands of the voters themselves. They alone can muster enough wisdom for the business, and they alone are without guile. The cure for the evils of democracy is more democracy.

All this, of course, is simply rhetoric. Every time anything of the kind is tried it fails ingloriously. Nor is there any evidence that it has ever succeeded elsewhere, to-day or in the past. Certainly no competent historian believes that the citizens assembled in a New England town-meeting actually formulated *en masse* the transcendental and immortal measures that they adopted, nor even that they contributed anything of value to the discussion thereof. The notion is as absurd as the parallel notion, long held by philologues of defective powers of observation, that the popular ballads surviving from earlier ages were actually composed by the folk.[1] The ballads, in point of fact, were all written by concrete poets, most of them not of the folk; the folk, when they had any hand in the business at all, simply acted as referees, choosing which should survive. In exactly the same way the New England town-meeting was led and dominated by a few men of unusual initiative and determination, some of them genuinely superior, but most of them simply demagogues and fanatics. The citizens in general heard the discussion of rival ideas, and went through the motions of deciding between them, but there is no evidence that they ever had all the relevant facts before them or made any effort to unearth them, or that appeals to their reason always, or even usually, prevailed over appeals to their mere prejudice and superstition. Their appetite for logic, I venture, seldom got the better of their fear of hell, and the Beatitudes moved them far less powerfully than blood. Some of the most idiotic decisions ever come to by mortal man were made by the New England town-meetings, and under the leadership of monomaniacs who are still looked upon as ineffable blossoms of the contemporary *Kultur*.[2]

The truth is that the difference between representative democracy and direct democracy is a great deal less marked than political sentimentalists assume. Under both forms the sovereign mob must employ agents to execute its will, and in either case the agents may have ideas of their own, based upon interests of their own, and the means at hand to do and get what they will. Moreover, their very position gives them a power of influencing the electors that is far above that of any ordinary citizen: they become politicians *ex officio*,[3] and usually end by selling such influence as remains after they have used all they need for their own ends. Worse, both forms of democracy encounter the difficulty that the generality of citizens, no matter how assiduously they may be instructed, remain congenitally unable to comprehend many of the problems before them, or to consider all of those they do comprehend in an unbiased and intelligent manner. Thus it is often impossible to ascertain their views in advance of action, or even, in many cases, to determine their conclusions *post hoc.*[4] The voters gathered in a typical New England town-meeting were all ardent amateurs of theology, and hence quite competent, in theory, to decide the theological questions that principally engaged them; nevertheless, history shows that they were led facilely by professional theologians, most of them quacks with something to sell. In the same way, the great masses of Americans of to-day, though they are theoretically competent to decide all the larger matters of national policy, and have certain immutable principles, of almost religious authority, to guide them, actually look for leading to professional politicians, who are influenced in turn by small but competent and determined minorities, with special knowledge and special interests. It was thus that the plain people were shoved into the late war, and it is thus that they will be shoved into the next one. They were, in overwhelming majority, against going in, and if they had had any sense and resolution they would have stayed out. But these things they lacked.

2.
The Popular Will

Thus there is no need to differentiate too pedantically between the two forms of democratic government, for their unlikeness is far more apparent than real. Nor is there any need to set up any distinction between the sort of democracy that is met with in practice, with its constant conflicts between what is assumed to be the popular will and the self-interest of small but articulate and efficient groups, and that theoretical variety which would liberate and energize the popular will completely. The latter must remain purely theoretical for all time; there are insuperable impediments, solidly grounded in the common mind, to its realization. Moreover, there is no reason for believing that its realization, if it should ever be attained by miracle, would materially change the main outlines of the democratic process. What is genuinely important is not that the will of mankind in the mass should be formulated and made effective at all times and in every case, but simply that means should be provided for ascertaining and executing it in capital cases—that there shall be no immovable impediment to its execution when, by some prodigy of nature, it takes a coherent and apposite form. If, over and beyond that, a sufficient sense of its immanent and imminent potency remains to make politicians walk a bit warily, if the threat always hangs in the air that under *x* circumstances and on *y* day it may be heard from suddenly and devastatingly, then democracy is actually in being. This is the case, it seems to me, in the United States. And it is the case, too, in every European country west of Vienna and north of the Alps.

The American people, true enough, are sheep. Worse, they are donkeys. Yet worse, to borrow from their own dialect, they are goats. They are thus constantly bamboozled and exploited by small minorities of their own number, by determined and ambitious individuals, and even by exterior groups. The business of victimizing them is a lucrative profession, an exact science, and a delicate and lofty art. It has its masters and it has its quacks. Its lowest reward is a seat in Congress or a job as a Prohibition agent, *i.e.*, a licensed blackleg; its highest reward is immortality. The adept practitioner is not only rewarded; he is also thanked. The victims delight in his ministrations, as an hypochondriacal woman delights in the flayings of the surgeon. But all the while they have the means in their hands to halt the obscenity whenever it becomes intolerable, and now and then, raised transiently to a sort of intelligence, they do put a stop to it. There are no legal or other bars to the free functioning of their will, once it emerges into consciousness, save only such bars as they themselves have erected, and these they may remove whenever they so desire. No external or super-legal power stands beyond their reach, exercising pressure upon them; they recognize no personal sovereign with inalienable rights and no class with privileges above the common law; they are even kept free, by a tradition as old as the Republic itself, of foreign alliances which would condition their autonomy. Thus their sovereignty, though it is limited in its everyday exercise by self-imposed constitutional checks and still more by restraints which lie in the very nature of government, whatever its form, is probably just as complete in essence as that of the most absolute monarch who ever hanged a peasant or defied the Pope.

What is too often forgotten, in discussing the matter, is the fact that no such monarch was ever actually free, at all times and under all conditions. In the midst of his most charming tyrannies he had still to bear it in mind that his people, oppressed too much, could always rise against him, and that he himself, though a king *von Gottes Gnaden,*[1] was yet biologically only a man, with but one gullet to slit; and if the people were feeble or too craven to be dangerous, then there was always His Holiness of Rome to fear or other agents of the King of Kings; and if these ghostly mentors, too, were silent, then he had to reckon with his ministers, his courtiers, his soldiers, his doctors, and his women. The Merovingian kings[2] were certainly absolute, if absolutism has ever existed outside the dreams of historians; nevertheless, as every schoolboy knows, their sovereignty was gradually undermined by the mayors of the palace, and finally taken from them altogether. So with the emperors of Japan, who succumbed to the shoguns, who succumbed in their turn to a combination of territorial nobles and city capitalists, not unlike that which brought King John[3] to bay at Runnymede. It seems to me that the common people, under such a democracy as that which now prevails in the United States, are more completely sovereign, in fact as well as in law, than any of these ancient despots. They may be seduced and enchained by a great variety of prehensile soothsayers, just as Henry VIII[4] was seduced and enchained by his wives, but, like Henry again, they are quite free to throw off their chains whenever they please, and to chop off the heads of their seducers. They could hang Dr. Coolidge[5] tomorrow if they really wanted to do it, or even Bishop Manning.[6] They could do it by the simple device of intimidating Congress, which never fails to leap when their growl is palpably in earnest. And if Congress stood out against them, they could do it anyhow, under protection of the jury system. The executioners, once acquitted, could not be molested more, save by illegal processes. Similar executioners walk the land to-day, especially in the South, and no one dares to challenge them. They are visible symbols of the powers that lie in the mob, once it makes up its mind.

Nor is there much force or relevancy in the contention that democracy is incomplete in the United States (as in England, France, Germany and all other democratic countries) because certain classes of persons are barred from full citizenship, sometimes for reasons that appear to be unsound. To argue thus is to argue against democracy itself, for if the majority has not the right to decide what qualifications shall be necessary to participate in its sovereignty, then it has no sovereignty at all. What one usually finds, on examining any given case of class disfranchisement, is that the class disfranchised is not actively eager, as a whole, for the ballot, and that its lack of interest in the matter is at least presumptive evidence of its general political incompetence. The three-class system of voting[7] survived so long in Belgium and Prussia, not because the masses victimized had no means at hand to put an end to it, but simply because they were so inept at politics, and so indifferent to the rights involved, that they made no genuine effort to do so. The agitation against the system was carried on mainly by a small minority, and many of its leaders were not even members of the class transgressed. Here we have a reminder of the process whereby democracy itself came in: it was forced upon its beneficiaries by a small group of visionaries, all of them standing outside the class benefited. So again, in our own time, with the extension of the franchise to women. The great masses of women in all countries were indifferent to the boon, and there was a considerable body that was cynically hostile. Perhaps a majority of the more ardent suffragists belonged biologically to neither sex.

Since the abolition of the three-class system in Prussia there has been absolutely no improvement in the government of that country; on the contrary, there has been a vast falling off in its honesty and efficiency, and it has even slackened energy in what was formerly one of its most laudable specialties: the development of legislation for the protection of the working class, *i.e.*, the very class that benefited politically by the change. Giving women the ballot, as everyone knows, has brought in none of the great reforms promised by the suffragists. It has substituted adultery for drunkenness as the principal divertissement at political conventions, but it has accomplished little else. The majority of women, when they vote at all, seem to vote unwillingly and without clear purpose; they are, perhaps, relatively too intelligent to have any faith in purely political remedies for the sorrows of the world. The minorities that show partisan keenness are chiefly made up of fat women with inattentive husbands; they are victimized easily by the male politicians, especially those who dress well, and are thus swallowed up by the great parties, and lose all separate effectiveness. Certainly it is usually difficult to discover, in the election returns, any division along anatomical lines. Now and then, true enough, a sentimentality appealing especially to the more stupid sort of women causes a transient differentiation, as when, for example, thousands of newly-enfranchised farm-wives in the United States voted against Cox, the Democratic presidential candidate, in 1920, on the double ground *(a)* that he was a divorcé and hence an antinomian,[8] and *(b)* that the titular chief of his party, Dr. Wilson, had married again too soon after the death of his first wife.[9] But such fantastic sentimentalities, after all, rarely enter into practical politics. When they are lacking the women voters simply succumb to the sentimentalities that happen to be engaging their lords and masters. The extension of the franchise has not changed the general nature of the political clown-show in the slightest. Campaigns are still made upon the same old issues, and offices go to the same old mountebanks, with a few Jezebels added to the corps to give it refinement.

There is little reason for believing that the extension of the franchise to the classes that still remain in the dark would make government more delicately responsive to the general will. Such classes, as a matter of fact, are now so few and so small in numbers in all of the Western nations that they may be very conveniently disregarded. It is as if doctors of philosophy, members of the Society of the Cincinnati[10] or men who could move their ears were disfranchised. In the United States, true enough, there is one disfranchised group that is much larger, to wit, that group of Americans whose African descent is visible to the naked eye and at a glance. But even in this case, the reality falls much below the appearance. The more intelligent American Negroes vote in spite of the opposition of the poor whites, their theological brothers and economic rivals, and not a few of them actually make their livings as professional politicians, even in the South. At the Republican National Convention at Chicago, in 1920, such a swart statesman gave an inspiring exhibition of his powers, and in the presence of a vast multitude. His name was Henry Lincoln Johnson,[11] and he has since gone to that bourn where black is white. When he died Dr. Coolidge sent a long and flirtatious telegram of condolence to his widow. The widow of Jacques Loeb[12] got no such telegram. This Johnson was chairman of the Georgia delegation, and his colleagues were all of the Nordic race. But though they came from the very citadel of the Ku Klux Klan,[13] he herded them in a public and lordly manner, and voted them as if they had been stuffed chemises. As Nordics, no doubt, they viewed him with a bitter loathing, but as politicians yearning for jobs they had to be polite to him, and even fawning. He has his peers and successors in all the American States. In many a proud city, North and South, the Aframericans hold the balance of power, and know it.

Moreover, even those who are actually disfranchised, say in the rural wastes of the South, may remove their disability by the simple device of moving away, as, in fact, hundreds of thousands have done. Their disfranchisement is thus not intrinsic and complete, but merely a function of their residence, like that of all persons, white or black, who live in the District of Columbia, and so it takes on a secondary and trivial character, as hay-fever, in the pathological categories, takes on a secondary and trivial character by yielding to a change of climate. Moreover, it is always extra-legal, and thus remains dubious: the theory of the fundamental law is that the coloured folk may and do vote. This theory they could convert into a fact at any time by determined mass action. The Nordics might resist that action, but they could not halt it: there would be another Civil War if they tried to do so, and they would be beaten a second time. If the blacks in the backwaters of the South keep away from the polls to-day it is only because they do not esteem the ballot highly enough to risk the dangers that go with trying to use it. That fact, it seems to me, convicts them of unfitness for citizenship in a democratic state, for the loftiest of all the rights of the citizen, by the democratic dogma, is that of the franchise, and whoever is not willing to fight for it, even at the cost of his last drop of gore, is surely not likely to exercise it with a proper sense of consecration after getting it. No one argues that democracy is destroyed in the United States by the fact that millions of white citizens, perfectly free under the law and the local *mores* of their communities to vote, nevertheless fail to do so. The difference between these negligent whites and the disfranchised Negroes is only superficial. Both have a clear legal right to the ballot; if they neglect to exercise it, it is only because they do not esteem it sufficiently. In New York City thousands of freeborn Caucasians surrender it in order to avoid jury duty; in the South thousands of Negroes surrender it in order to avoid having their homes burned and their heads broken. The two motives are fundamentally identical; in each case the potential voter values his peace and security more than he values the boon for which the Fathers bled. He certainly has a right to choose.

3.
Disproportional Representation

The matter of disproportional representation, already alluded to in connection with the Prussian-Belgian voting system, is intimately bound up with this question of disfranchised classes, for it must be plain that a community whose votes, man for man, count for only half as much as the votes of another community is one in which half of the citizens are, to every practical intent, unable to vote at all. As everyone knows, the United States Senate is constituted upon a disproportional plan. Each State, regardless of population, has two Senators and no more, and the votes of the two representing so small and measly a State as Delaware or Nevada count for precisely as much as the votes of the Senators from Pennsylvania or New York. The same sophistication of the one-man-one-vote formula extends into the States themselves. There is hardly a large city in the United States that has completely proportional representation in the State Legislature. In almost every State, sometimes with slight ameliorative differences, the Upper house of the Legislature is constituted upon the plan of the Federal Senate—that is, the divisions run according to geographical boundaries rather than according to population, and the congested urban centres tend to be grossly under-represented. Moreover, the lower house commonly shows something of the same disharmony, even when it is ostensibly based upon proportional representation, for the cities grow in population much faster than the country districts, and reapportionment always lags behind that growth.

These facts fever certain romantic fuglemen of so-called pure democracy, and they come forward with complicated remedies, all of which have been tried somewhere or other and failed miserably. The truth is that disproportional representation is not a device to nullify democracy, but simply a device to make it more workable. All it indicates, at least in the United States, is that the sovereign people have voluntarily sacrificed a moiety of the democratic theory in order to attain to a safer and more efficient practice. If they so desired they could sweep all of the existing inequalities out of existence—not instantly, perhaps, but nevertheless surely. Every such inequality is founded upon their free will, and nearly every one enjoys their complete approval. What lies under most of them is not a wish to give one voter an advantage over another, but a wish to counter-balance an advantage lying in the very nature of things. The voters of a large urban centre, for example, are able to act together far more promptly and effectively than their colleagues of the wide-flung farms. They live in close contact both physically and mentally; opinions form among them quickly, and are maintained with solid front. In brief, they show all of the characters of men in a compact mob, and the voters of the rural regions, dispersed and largely inarticulate, cannot hope to prevail against them by ordinary means. So the yokels are given disproportionally heavy representation by way of make-weight: it enables them to withstand the city stampede. There are frequent protests from the cities when, taking advantage of their strength in the State Legislatures, the yokels dodge their fair share of the burden of taxation, but it is perhaps significant that there is seldom any serious protest against the plan of organization of the United States Senate, despite the fact that it has cursed the country with such bucolic imbecilities as Prohibition. In both cases, genuine discontent would make itself felt, for the majority under democracy remains the majority, whatever laws and constitutions may say to the contrary, and when its blood is up it can get anything it wants.

Most of the so-called constitutional checks, in fact, have yielded, at one time or other, to its pressure. No one familiar with the history of the Supreme Court, for example, need be told that its vast and singular power to curb legislation has always been exercised with one eye on the election returns. Practically all of its most celebrated decisions, from that in the Dred Scott case[1] to that in the Northern Securities case,[2] have reflected popular rages of the hour, and many of them have been modified, or even completely reversed afterward, as the second thought of the plain people has differed from their first thought. This responsiveness to the shifts of popular opinion and passion is not alone due to the fact that the personnel of the court, owing to the high incidence of senile deterioration among its members, is constantly changing, and that the President and the Senators, in filling vacancies, are bound as practical politicians to consider the doctrines that happen to be fashionable in the cross-roads grocery-stores and barber-shops. It is also due, and in no small measure, to the fact that the learned and puissant justices are, in the main, practical politicians themselves, and hence used to keeping their ears close to the grass-roots. Most of them, before they were elevated to the ermine, spent years struggling desperately for less exalted honours, and so, like Representatives, Senators and Presidents, they show a fine limberness of the *biceps femoris, semitendinosus* and *semimembranosus,*[3] and a beautiful talent for reconciling the ideally just with the privately profitable. If their general tendency, in late years, has been to put the rights of property above the rights of man then it must be obvious that they have not lost any popularity thereby. In boom times, indeed, democracy is always very impatient of what used to be called natural rights. The typical democrat is quite willing to exchange any of the theoretical boons of freedom for something that he can use. In most cases, perhaps, he is averse to selling his vote for cash in hand, but that is mainly because the price offered is usually too low. He will sell it very willingly for a good job or for some advantage in his business. Offering him such bribes, in fact, is the chief occupation of all political parties under democracy, and of all professional politicians.

For all these reasons I esteem it a vanity to discuss the question whether the democracy on tap in the United States is really ideal. Ideal or not, it works, and the people are actually sovereign. The governmental process, perhaps, could be made more quickly responsive to the public will, but that is merely a temporal detail; it is responsive enough for all practical purposes. Any conceivable change in the laws could be effected without tampering with the fundamental scheme. The fact, no doubt, largely explains the hostility of the inferior American to the thing called direct action—the darling of his equals in most other countries. He is against it, not merely because he is a coward and distrusts liberty, but also, and maybe mainly, because he believes that revolution, in the United States, is unnecessary—that any reform advocated by a respectable majority, or even by a determined minority, may be achieved peacefully and by constitutional means. In this belief he is right. The American people, keeping strictly within the Constitution, could do anything that the most soaring fancy suggested. They could, by a simple amendment of that hoary scripture, expropriate all the private property in the land, or they could expropriate parts of it and leave the rest in private hands; they have already, in fact, by tariff juggling, by Prohibition and by other devices, destroyed billions of dollars of property without compensation and even without common politeness, and the Constitution still survives. They could enfranchise aliens if they so desired, or children not taxed, or idiots, or the kine in the byres.[4] They could disfranchise whole classes, *e.g.*, metaphysicians or adulterers, or the entire population of given regions. They have done such things. They could abolish the Federal and State Legislatures, as they have already abolished the city councils in hundreds of municipalities. They could extend the term of the President to life, or they could reduce it to one year, or even to one day. They could provide that he must shave his head, or that he must sleep in his underclothes. They could legalize his assassination for malfeasance, and the assassination of all other recreant public officers, as I myself once proposed,[5] entirely within my rights as a citizen and a patriot. They could introduce burning at the stake, flogging, castration, ducking and tar-and-feathering into our system of legal punishment; they have already done so in the South by acclamation, regardless of the law and the courts, and, as the phrase is, have got away with it. They could abolish the jury system, abandon the writ of *habeas corpus,* authorize unreasonable searches and seizures, legalize murder by public officers and provide that all Federal judges be appointed by the Anti-Saloon League[6]: a beginning has been made in all these fields by the Volstead Act.[7] They could make war without constitutional authority and refuse to engage in it in the face of a constitutional declaration. They could proscribe individuals or classes, and deny them the protection of the laws. They could convert arson into a laudable act, provide a bounty for persons skilled at mayhem and make it a crime to drink coffee or eat meat. They have already,[8] either by Federal action or by State action, made crimes of such intrinsically harmless acts as drinking wine at meals, smoking cigarettes on the street, teaching the elements of biology, wearing a red necktie on the street, and reading "Das Kapital" and "The Inestimable Life of the Great Gargantua."[9] They could, with equal facility, make it criminal to refuse to do these things. Finally, they could, if they would, abandon the republican form of government altogether, and set up a monarchy in place of it; during the late war they actually did so in fact, though refraining from saying so frankly. They could do all of these things freely and even legally, without departing in the slightest from the principles of their fundamental compact, and no exterior agency could make them do any of them unwillingly.

It is thus idle to amass proofs, as Hans Delbrück[10] does with great diligence, that the result of this or that election was not a manifestation of a concrete popular wish. The answer, nine times out of ten, is that there *was* no popular wish. The populace simply passed over the matters principally at issue as incomprehensible or unimportant, and voted irrelevantly or wantonly. Or, in large part, it kept away from the polls. Both actions might be defended plausibly by democratic theorists. The people, if they are actually sovereign, have a clear right to be wanton when the spirit moves them, and indifference to an issue is an expression of opinion about it. Thus there is little appositeness in the saying of another German, the philosopher Hegel,[11] that the masses are that part of the state which doesn't know what it wants. They know what they want when they actually want it, and if they want it badly enough they get it. What they want principally are safety and security. They want to be delivered from the bugaboos that ride them. They want to be soothed with mellifluous words. They want heroes to worship. They want the rough entertainment suitable to their simple minds. All of these things they want so badly that they are willing to sacrifice everything else in order to get them. The science of politics under democracy consists in trading with them, *i.e.*, in hoodwinking and swindling them. In return for what they want, or for the mere appearance of what they want, they yield up what the politician wants, and what the enterprising minorities behind him want. The bargaining is conducted to the tune of affecting rhetoric, with music by the choir, but it is as simple and sordid at bottom as the sale of a mule. It lies quite outside the bounds of honour, and even of common decency. It is a combat between jackals and jackasses. It is the master transaction of democratic states.

4.
The Politician Under Democracy

I find myself quoting yet a third German: he is Professor Robert Michels,[1] the economist. The politician, he says, is the courtier of democracy. A profound saying—perhaps more profound than the professor, himself a democrat, realizes. For it was of the essence of the courtier's art and mystery that he flattered his employer in order to victimize him, yielded to him in order to rule him. The politician under democracy does precisely the same thing. His business is never what it pretends to be. Ostensibly he is an altruist devoted whole-heartedly to the service of his fellow-men, and so abjectly public-spirited that his private interest is nothing to him. Actually he is a sturdy rogue whose principal, and often sole aim in life is to butter his parsnips. His technical equipment consists simply of an armamentarium of deceits. It is his business to get and hold his job at all costs.

If he can hold it by lying he will hold it by lying; if lying peters out he will try to hold it by embracing new truths. His ear is ever close to the ground. If he is an adept he can hear the first murmurs of popular clamour before even the people themselves are conscious of them. If he is a master he detects and whoops up today the delusions that the mob will cherish next year. There is in him, in his professional aspect, no shadow of principle or honour. It is moral by his code to get into office by false pretences, as the late Dr. Wilson did in 1916. It is moral to change convictions overnight, as multitudes of American politicians did when the Prohibition avalanche came down upon them. Anything is moral that furthers the main concern of his soul, which is to keep a place at the public trough. That place is one of public honour, and public honour is the thing that caresses him and makes him happy. It is also one of power, and power is the commodity that he has for sale.

I speak here, of course, of the democratic politician in his role of statesman—that is, in his best and noblest aspect. He flourishes also on lower levels, partly subterranean. Down there public honour would be an inconvenience, so he hawks it to lesser men, and contents himself with power. What are the sources of that power? They lie, obviously, in the gross weaknesses and knaveries of the common people—in their inability to grasp any issues save the simplest and most banal, in their incurable tendency to fly into preposterous alarms, in their petty self-seeking and venality, in their instinctive envy and hatred of their superiors—in brief, in their congenital incapacity for the elemental duties of citizens in a civilized state. The boss owns them simply because they can be bought for a job on the street or a load of coal. He holds them, even when they pass beyond any need of jobs or coal, by his shrewd understanding of their immemorial sentimentalities. Looking at Thersites,[2] they see Ulysses.[3] He is the state as they apprehend it; around him clusters all the romance that used to hang about a king. He is the fount of honour and the mould of form. His barbaric code, framed to fit their gullibility, becomes an example to their young. The boss is the eternal *reductio ad absurdum*[4] of the whole democratic process. He exemplifies its reduction of all ideas to a few elemental wants. And he reflects and makes manifest the inferior man's congenital fear of liberty—his incapacity for even the most trivial sort of independent action. Life on the lower levels is life in a series of interlocking despotisms. The inferior man cannot imagine himself save as taking orders—if not from the boss, then from the priest, and if not from the priest, then from some fantastic drill-sergeant of his own creation. For years the reformers who flourished in the United States concentrated their whole animus upon the boss: it was apparently their notion that he had imposed himself upon his victims from without, and that they could be delivered by destroying him. But time threw a brilliant light upon that error. When, as and if he was overthrown there appeared in his place the prehensile Methodist parson, bawling for Prohibition and its easy jobs, and behind the parson loomed the grand goblin, natural heir to a long line of imperial worthy potentates of the Sons of Azrael and sublime chancellors of the Order of Patriarchs Militant.[5] The winds of the world are bitter to *Homo vulgaris*.[6] He likes the warmth and safety of the herd, and he likes a bell-wether with a clarion bell.

The art of politics, under democracy, is simply the art of ringing it. Two branches reveal themselves. There is the art of the demagogue, and there is the art of what may be called, by a shot-gun marriage of Latin and Greek, the demaslave. They are complementary, and both of them are degrading to their practitioners. The demagogue is one who preaches doctrines he knows to be untrue to men he knows to be idiots. The demaslave is one who listens to what these idiots have to say and then pretends that he believes it himself. Every man who seeks elective office under democracy has to be either the one thing or the other, and most men have to be both. The whole process is one of false pretences and ignoble concealments. No educated man, stating plainly the elementary notions that every educated man holds about the matters that principally concern government, could be elected to office in a democratic state, save perhaps by a miracle. His frankness would arouse fears, and those fears would run against him; it is his business to arouse fears that will run in favour of him. Worse, he must not only consider the weaknesses of the mob, but also the prejudices of the minorities that prey upon it. Some of these minorities have developed a highly efficient technique of intimidation. They not only know how to arouse the fears of the mob; they also know how to awaken its envy, its dislike of privilege, its hatred of its betters. How formidable they may become is shown by the example of the Anti-Saloon League in the United States—a minority body in the strictest sense, however skillful its mustering of popular support, for it nowhere includes a majority of the voters among its subscribing members, and its leaders are nowhere chosen by democratic methods. And how such minorities may intimidate the whole class of place-seeking politicians has been demonstrated brilliantly and obscenely by the same corrupt and unconscionable organization. It has filled all the law-making bodies of the nation with men who have got into office by submitting cravenly to its dictation, and it has filled thousands of administrative posts, and not a few judicial posts, with vermin of the same sort.

Such men, indeed, enjoy vast advantages under democracy. The mob, insensitive to their dishonour, is edified and exhilarated by their success. The competition they offer to men of a decenter habit is too powerful to be met, so they tend, gradually, to monopolize all the public offices. Out of the muck of their swinishness the typical American law-maker emerges. He is a man who has lied and dissembled, and a man who has crawled. He knows the taste of boot-polish. He has suffered kicks in the tonneau of his pantaloons. He has taken orders from his superiors in knavery and he has wooed and flattered his inferiors in sense. His public life is an endless series of evasions and false pretences. He is willing to embrace any issue, however idiotic, that will get him votes, and he is willing to sacrifice any principle, however sound, that will lose them for him. I do not describe the democratic politician at his inordinate worst; I describe him as he is encountered in the full sunshine of normalcy. He may be, on the one hand, a cross-roads idler striving to get into the State Legislature by grace of the local mortgage-sharks and evangelical clergy, or he may be, on the other, the President of the United States. It is almost an axiom that no man may make a career in politics in the Republic without stooping to such ignobility: it is as necessary as a loud voice. Now and then, to be sure, a man of sounder self-respect may make a beginning, but he seldom gets very far. Those who survive are nearly all tarred, soon or late, with the same stick. They are men who, at some time or other, have compromised with their honour, either by swallowing their convictions or by whooping for what they believe to be untrue. They are in the position of the chorus girl who, in order to get her humble job, has had to admit the manager to her person. And the old birds among them, like chorus girls of long experience, come to regard the business resignedly and even complacently. It is the price that a man who loves the clapper-clawing of the vulgar must pay for it under the democratic system. He becomes a coward and a trimmer *ex officio.* Where his dignity was in the days of his innocence there is now only a vacuum in the wastes of his subconscious. Vanity remains to him, but not pride.

5.
Utopia

Thus the ideal of democracy is reached at last: it has become a psychic impossibility for a gentleman to hold office under the Federal Union, save by a combination of miracles that must tax the resourcefulness even of God. The fact has been rammed home by a constitutional amendment: every office-holder, when he takes oath to support the Constitution, must swear on his honour that, summoned to the death-bed of his grandmother, he will not take the old lady a bottle of wine. He may say so and do it, which makes him a liar, or he may say so and not do it, which makes him a pig. But despite that grim dilemma there are still idealists, chiefly professional Liberals, who argue that it is the duty of a gentleman to go into politics—that there is a way out of the quagmire in that direction. The remedy, it seems to me, is quite as absurd as all the other sure cures that Liberals advocate. When they argue for it, they simply argue, in words but little changed, that the remedy for prostitution is to fill the bawdyhouses with virgins. My impression is that this last device would accomplish very little: either the virgins would leap out of the windows, or they would cease to be virgins. The same alternatives confront the political aspirant who is what is regarded in America as a gentleman—that is, who is one not susceptible to open bribery in cash. The moment his leg goes over the political fence, he finds the mob confronting him, and if he would stay within he must adapt himself to its tastes and prejudices. In other words, he must learn all the tricks of the regular mountebanks. When the mob pricks up its ears and begins to whinny, he must soothe it with balderdash. He must allay its resentment of the fact that he is washed behind the ears. He must anticipate its crazes, and join in them vociferously. He must regard its sensitiveness on points of morals, and get what advantage he can out of his anaesthesia on points of honour. More, he must make terms with the mob-masters already performing upon its spines, chiefly agents of prehensile minorities. If he neglects these devices he is swiftly heaved over the fence, and his career in statecraft is at an end.

Here I do not theorize; there are examples innumerable. It is an axiom of practical politics, indeed, that the worst enemies of political decency are the tired reformers—and the worst of the worst are those whose primary thirst to make the corruptible put on incorruption was accompanied by a somewhat sniffish class consciousness. Has the United States ever seen a more violent and shameless demagogue than Theodore Roosevelt? Yet Roosevelt came into politics as a sword drawn against demagogy. The list of such recusants might be run to great lengths: I point to the late Mitchel of New York[1] and the late Lodge of Massachusetts[2] and pass on. Lodge lived long enough to become a magnificent *reductio ad absurdum* of the gentleman turned democratic messiah. It was a sheer impossibility, during the last ten years of his life, to disentangle his private convictions from the fabric of his political dodges. He was the perfect model of the party hack, and if he performed before the actual mob less unchastely than Roosevelt it was only because his somewhat absurd façade unfitted him for that science. He dealt in jobs in a wholesale manner, and with the hearty devotion of a Penrose[3] or a Henry Lincoln Johnson.[4] Popularly regarded as an unflinching and even adamantine fellow, he was actually as limber as an eel. He knew how to jump. He knew when to whisper and when to yell. As I say, I could print a long roster of similar apostates; the name of Penrose himself should not be forgotten. I do not say that a gentleman may not thrust himself into politics under democracy; I simply say that it is almost impossible for him to stay there and remain a gentleman. The haughty amateur, at the start, may actually make what seems to be a brilliant success, for he is commonly full of indignation, and so strikes out valiantly, and the mob crowds up because it likes a brutal show. But that first battle is almost always his last. If he retains his rectitude he loses his office, and if he retains his office he has to dilute his rectitude with the cologne spirits of the trade.

Such is the price* that we pay for the great boon of democracy: the man of native integrity is either barred from the public service altogether, or subjected to almost irresistible temptations after he gets in. The competition of less honourable man is more than he can bear. He must stand against them before the mob, and the sempiternal prejudices of the mob run their way. In most other countries of a democratic tendency—for example, England—this outlawry and corruption of the best is checked by an aristocratic tradition—an anachronism, true enough, but still extremely powerful, and yielding to the times only under immense pressure. The English aristocracy (aided, in part, by the plutocracy, which admires and envies it) not only keeps a large share of the principal offices in its own hands, regardless of popular rages and party fortunes; it also preserves an influence, and hence a function, for its non-officeholding members. The scholarship of Oxford and Cambridge, for example, can still make itself felt at Westminster, despite the fact that the vast majority of the actual members of the Commons are ignoramuses. But in the United States there is no aristocracy, whether intellectual or otherwise, and so the scholarship of Harvard, such as it is, is felt no more on Capitol Hill than it is at Westerville, Ohio.[5] The class of politicians, indeed, tends to separate itself sharply from all other classes. There is none of that interpenetration on the higher levels which marks older and more secure societies. Roosevelt, an imitation aristocrat,[6] was the first and only American President since Washington to make any effort to break down the barriers.

*Correcting "pride" in original text.

A man of saucy and even impertinent curiosities, and very eager to appear to the vulgar as an Admirable Crichton,[7] he made his table the resort of all sorts and conditions of men. Among them were some who actually knew something about this or that, and from them he probably got useful news and advice. Beethoven, if he had been alive, would have been invited to the White House, and Goethe[8] would have come with him. But that eagerness for contacts outside the hounds of professional politics is certainly not a common mark of American Presidents, nor, of American public officials of any sort. When the lamented Harding sat in Lincoln's chair his hours of ease were spent with bootleggers, not with metaphysicians; his notion of a good time was to refresh himself in the manner of a small-town Elk,[9] at golf, poker, and guzzling. The tastes of his successor are even narrower: the loftiest guests he entertains upon the *Mayflower*[10] are the editors of party newspapers, and there is no evidence that he is acquainted with a single intelligent man. The average American Governor is of the same kidney. He comes into contact with the local *Gelehrte*[11] only when a bill is up to prohibit the teaching of the elements of biology in the State university.

The judiciary, under the American system, sinks quite as low. Save when, by some miscarriage of politics, a Brandeis, a Holmes, a Cardozo or a George W. Anderson[12] is elevated to the bench, it carries on its dull and preposterous duties quite outside the stream of civilized thought, and even outside the stream of enlightened juridic thought. Very few American judges ever contribute anything of value to legal theory. One seldom hears of them protesting, either *ex cathedra*[13] or as citizens, against the extravagances and absurdities that fast reduce the whole legal system of the country to imbecility; they seem to be quite content to enforce any sort of law that is provided for their use by ignorant and corrupt legislators, regardless of its conflict with fundamental human rights. The Constitution apparently has no more meaning to them than it has to a Prohibition agent. They have acquiesced almost unanimously in the destruction of the First, Second, Fourth, Fifth and Sixth Amendments, and supinely connived at the invasion of the Fourteenth and Fifteenth.[14] The reason is not far to seek. The average American judge, in his days at the bar, was not a leader but a trailer. The judicial office is not attractive, as a rule, to the better sort of lawyers. We have such a multiplicity of courts that it has become common, and judges are so often chosen for purely political reasons, even for the Supreme Court of the United States, that the lawyer of professional dignity and self-respect hesitates to enter into the competition. Thus the bench tends to be filled with duffers, and many of them are also scoundrels, as the frequent complaints against their extortions and tyrannies testify. The English bench, as everyone knows, is immensely better: the fact is often noted with lamentation by American lawyers. And why? Simply because the governing oligarchy in England, lingering on in spite of the democratic upheaval, keeps jealous guard over the judiciary in the interest of its own class, and thereby prevents the elevation of the preposterous shysters who so frequently attain to the ermine in America. Even when, under the pressure of parlous times, it admits an F. E. Smith[15] to the bench, it at least makes sure that he is a competent lawyer. The way is thus blocked to downright ignoramuses, and English jurisprudence, so much more fluent and reasonable than our own, is protected against their dull stupidities. Genuine talent, however humble its origin, may get in, but not imbecilitly, however pretentious. In the United States the thing runs the other way. In the States, where judges are commonly elected by popular vote, the shyster has every advantage over the reputable lawyer, including that of yearning for the judicial salary with a vast and undivided passion. And when it comes to the Federal courts, once so honourable, he has every advantage again, including the formidable one of knowing how to crook his knee gracefully to the local dispenser of Federal patronage (in the South, often a worthless Negro) and to the Methodist wowsers of the Anti-Saloon League.

6.
The Occasional Exception

I do not argue, of course, that the shyster invariably prevails. As I have said, a man of unquestionable integrity and ability occasionally gets to the bench, even of the State courts. In the same way a man of unquestionable integrity and ability sometimes finds himself in high executive or legislative office; there are even a few cases of such men getting into the White House. But the thing doesn't happen often, and when it does happen it is only by a failure of the rule. The self-respecting candidate obviously cannot count on that failure: the odds are heavily against him from the start, and every effort he makes to diminish them involves some compromise with complete candour. He may take refuge in cynicism, and pursue the cozening of the populace as a sort of intellectual exercise, cruel but not unamusing, or he may accept the conditions of the game resignedly, and charge up the necessary dodges and false pretences to spiritual profit and loss, as a chorus girl charges up her favours to the manager and his backer; but in either case he has parted with something that must be tremendously valuable to a self-respecting man, and is even more valuable to the country he serves than it is to himself. Contemplating such a body as the national House of Representatives one sees only a group of men who have compromised with honour—in brief, a group of male Magdalens. They have been broken to the goose-step. They have learned how to leap through the hoops of professional job-mongers and Prohibitionist blackmailers. They have kept silent about good causes, and spoken in causes that they knew to be evil. The higher they rise, the further they fall. The occasional mavericks, thrown in by miracle, last a session, and then disappear. The old Congressman, the veteran of genuine influence and power, is either one who is so stupid that the ideas of the mob are his own ideas, or one so far gone in charlatanry that he is unconscious of his shame. Our laws are made, in the main, by men who have sold their honour for their jobs, and they are executed by men who put their jobs above justice and common sense. The occasional cynics leaven the mass. We are dependent for whatever good flows out of democracy upon men who do not believe in democracy.

Here, perhaps, it will be urged that my argument goes beyond the democratic scheme and lodges against government itself. There is, I believe, some cogency in the caveat. All government, whatever its form, is carried on chiefly by men whose first concern is for their offices, not for their obligations. It is, in its essence, a conspiracy of a small group against the masses of men, and especially against the masses of diligent and useful men. Its primary aim is to keep this group in jobs that are measurably more comfortable and exhilarating than the jobs its members could get in free competition. They are thus always willing to make certain sacrifices of integrity and self-respect in order to hold those jobs, and the fact is just as plain under a despot as it is under the mob. The mob has its flatterers and bosh-mongers; the king has his courtiers. But there is yet a difference, and I think it is important. The courtier, at his worst, at least performs his genuflections before one who is theoretically his superior, and is surely not less than his equal. He does not have to abase himself before swine with whom, ordinarily, he would disdain to have any traffic. He is not compelled to pretend that he is a worse man than he really is. He needn't hold his nose in order to approach his benefactor. Thus he may go into office without having dealt his honour a fatal wound, and once he is in, he is under no pressure to sacrifice it further, and may nurse it back to health and vigour. His sovereign, at worst, has a certain respect for it, and hesitates to strain it unduly; the mob has no sensitiveness on that point, and, indeed, no knowledge that it exists. The courtier's sovereign, in other words, is apt to be a man of honour himself. When, in 1848 or thereabout, the late Wilhelm I of Prussia[1] was offered the imperial crown by a so-called parliament of his subjects, he refused it on the ground that he could take it only from his equals, *i.e.*, from the sovereign princes of the *Reich.*[2] To the democrats of the world this attitude was puzzling, and on reflection it began to seem contemptible and offensive. But that was not to be marveled at. To a democrat any attitude based upon a concept of honour, dignity and integrity seems contemptible and offensive. Once Frederick the Great was asked why he gave commissions in his army only to *Junker.*[3] Because, he answered, they will not lie and they cannot be bought. That answer explains sufficiently the general democratic theory that the *Junker* are not only scoundrels, but also half-wits.

The democratic politician, facing such plain facts, tries to save his *amour propre*[4] in a characteristically human way; that is to say, he denies them. We all do that. We convert our degradations into renunciations, our self-seeking into public spirit, our swinishness into heroism. No man, I suppose, ever admits to himself candidly that he gets his living in a dishonourable way, not even a Prohibition agent or a biter off of puppies' tails. The democratic politician, confronted by the dishonesty and stupidity of his master, the mob, tries to convince himself and all the rest of us that it is really full of rectitude and wisdom. This is the origin of the doctrine that, whatever its transient errors, it always comes to right decisions in the long run. Perhaps—but on what evidence, by what reasoning, and for what motives! Go examine the long history of the anti-slavery agitation in America: it is a truly magnificent record of buncombe, false pretences, and imbecility. This notion that the mob is wise, I fear, is not to be taken seriously: it was invented by mob-masters to save their faces: there was a lot of chatter about it by Roosevelt, but none by Washington, and very little by Jefferson. Whenever democracy, by an accident, produces a genuine statesman, he is found to be proceeding on the assumption that it is not true. And on the assumption that it is difficult, if not impossible to go to the mob for support, and still retain the ordinary decencies. The best democratic statesmanship, like the best non-democratic statesmanship, tends to safeguard the honour of the higher officers of state by relieving them of that degrading necessity. As every schoolboy knows, such was the intent of the Fathers, as expressed in Article II, Sections 1 and 2, of the Constitution.[5] To this day it is a common device, when this or that office becomes steeped in intolerable corruption, to take it out of the gift of the mob, and make it appointive. The aspirant, of course, still has to seek it, for under democracy it is very rare that office seeks the man, but seeking it of the President, or even of the Governor of a State, is felt to be appreciably less humiliating and debasing than seeking it of the mob. The President may be a Coolidge, and the Governor may be a Blease[6] or a Ma Ferguson,[7] but he (or she) is at least able to understand plain English, and need not he put into good humour by the arts of the circus clown or Baptist evangelist.

To sum up: the essential objection to feudalism (the perfect antithesis to democracy) was that it imposed degrading acts and attitudes upon the vassal; the essential objection to democracy is that, with few exceptions, it imposes degrading acts and attitudes upon the men responsible for the welfare and dignity of the state. The former was compelled to do homage to his suzerain, who was very apt to be a brute and an ignoramus. The latter are compelled to do homage to their constituents, who in overwhelming majority are certain to be both.

7.
The Maker of Laws

In the United States, the general democratic tendency to crowd competent and self-respecting men out of the public service is exaggerated by a curious constitutional rule, unknown in any other country. This is the rule, embodied in Article I, Sections 2 and 3, of the Constitution and carried over into most of the State constitutions, that a legislator must be an actual resident of the district he represents. Its obvious aim is to preserve for every electoral unit a direct and continuous voice in the government; its actual effect is to fill all the legislative bodies of the land with puerile local politicians, many of them so stupid that they are quite unable to grasp the problems with which government has to deal. In England it is perfectly possible for the remotest division to choose a Morley[1] to represent it, and this, in fact, until the recent rise of the mob, was not infrequently done. But in the United States every congressional district must find its representative within its own borders, and only too often there is no competent man available. Even if one happens to live there—which in large areas of the South and many whole States of the newer West, is extremely improbable—he is usually so enmeshed in operations against the resident imbeciles and their leaders, and hence so unpopular, that his candidacy is out of the question. This is manifestly the case in such States as Tennessee and Mississippi. Neither is without civilized inhabitants, but in neither is it possible to find a civilized inhabitant who is not under the ban of the local Fundamentalist clergy, and *per corollary*, of the local politicians. Thus both States, save for occasional accidents, are represented in Congress by delegations of pliant and unconscionable jackasses, and their influence upon national legislation is extremely evil. It was the votes of such ignoble fellows, piling in from all the more backward States, that forced the Eighteenth Amendment[2] through both Houses of Congress, and it was the votes of even more degraded noodles, assembled from the backwoods in the State Legislatures, that put the amendment into the Constitution.

If it were possible for a congressional district to choose any man to represent it, as is the case in all other civilized countries, there would be more breaks in the monotony of legislative venality and stupidity, for even the rustic mob, in the absence of strong local antipathies, well fanned by demagogues, might succumb occasionally to the magic of a great name. Thus a Roscoe Pound[3] might be sent to Congress from North Dakota or Nevada, though it is obvious that he could not be sent from the Massachusetts district in which he lives, wherein his independence and intelligence are familiar and hence offensive to his neighbours. But this is forbidden by the constitutional rule, and so North Dakota and Nevada, with few if any first-rate men in them, must turn to such men as they have. The result everywhere is the election of a depressing gang of incompetents, mainly petty lawyers and small-town bankers. The second result is a House of Representatives that, in intelligence, information and integrity, is comparable to a gang of bootleggers—a House so deficient in competent leaders that it can scarcely carry on its business. The third result is the immense power of such corrupt and sinister agencies as the Anti-Saloon League: a Morley would disdain its mandates, but Congressman John J. Balderdash[4] is only too eager to earn its support at home. A glance through the Congressional Directory, which prints autobiographies (often full of voluptuous self-praise) of all Congressmen, is enough to show what scrub stock is in the Lower House. The average Southern member, for example, runs true to a standard type. He got his early education in a hedge school,[5] he proceeded to some preposterous Methodist or Baptist college, and then he served for a time as a schoolteacher in his native swamps, finally reaching the dignity of county superintendent of schools and meanwhile reading law. Admitted to the bar, and having got a taste of county politics as superintendent, he became district attorney, and perhaps, after a while, county judge. Then he began running for Congress, and after three or four vain attempts, finally won a seat. The unfitness of such a man for the responsibilities of a law-maker must he obvious. He is an ignoramus, and he is quite without the common decencies. Having to choose between sense and nonsense, he chooses nonsense almost instinctively. Until he got to Washington, and began to meet lobbyists, bootleggers and the correspondents of the newspapers, he had perhaps never met a single intelligent human being. As a Congressman, he remains below the salt.[6] Officialdom disdains him; he is kept waiting in anterooms by all the fourth assistant secretaries. When he is invited to a party, it is a sign that police sergeants are also invited. He must be in his second or third term before the ushers at the White House so much as remember his face. His dream is to be chosen to go on a congressional junket, *i.e.*, on a drunken holiday at government expense. His daily toil is getting jobs for relatives and retainers. Sometimes he puts a dummy[7] on the pay-roll and collects the dummy's salary himself. In brief, a knavish and preposterous nonentity, half way between a kleagle of the Ku Klux and a grand worthy bow-wow of the Knights of Zoroaster.[8] It is such vermin who make the laws of the United States.

The gentlemen of the Upper House are measurably better, if only because they serve for longer terms. A Congressman, with his two-year term, is constantly running for re-election. Scarcely has he got to Washington before he must hurry home and resume his bootlicking of the local bosses. But a Senator, once sworn in, may safely forget them for two or three years, and so, if there is no insuperable impediment in his character, he may show a certain independence, and yet survive. Moreover, he is usually safer than a Congressman, even as his term ends, for his possession of a higher office shows that he is no inconsiderable boss himself. Thus there are Senators who attain to a laudable mastery of the public business, particularly such as lies within the range of their private interests, and even Senators who show the intellectual dignity and vigour of genuine statesmen. But they are surely not numerous. The average Senator, like the average Congressman, is simply a party hack, without ideas and without anything rationally describable as self-respect. His backbone has a sweet resiliency; he knows how to clap on false whiskers; it is quite impossible to forecast his action, even on a matter of the highest principle, without knowing what rewards are offered by the rival sides. Two of the most pretentious Senators, during the Sixty-Ninth Congress, were the gentlemen from Pennsylvania: one of them, indeed, was the successor to the lamented Henry Cabot Lodge as the intellectual snob of the Upper House.[9] Yet both, under pressure, performed such dizzy flops that even the Senate gasped. It was amusing, but there was also a touch of pathos in it. Here were men who plainly preferred their jobs to their dignity. Here, in brief, were men whose private rectitude had yielded to political necessity—the eternal tragedy of democracy. I turn to the testimony of a Senator who stands out clearly from the rest; the able and uncompromisingly independent Reed of Missouri.[10] This is what he said of his colleagues, to their faces, on June 2, 1924[11]:

> [The pending measure] will be voted for by cowards who would rather hang on to their present offices than serve their country or defend its Constitution. It would not receive a vote in this body were there not many individuals looking over their shoulders toward the ballot-boxes of November, their poltroon souls aquiver with apprehension lest they may pay the price of courageous duty

> by the loss of the votes of some *bloc,* clique, or coterie backing this infamous proposal. My language may seem brutal. If so, it is because it lays on the blistering truth.

Senator Reed, in this startling characterization of his fellow Senators, plainly violated the rules of the Senate, which forbid one member to question the motives of another. But there was no Senator present that day who cared to invoke those rules. They all knew that Reed told the truth. Their answer to him was to slink into the cloak-rooms, and leave him to roar at the Vice-President and the clerks. He not only described the Senate accurately; he also described the whole process of law-making under democracy. Our laws are invented, in the main, by frauds and fanatics, and put upon the statute books by poltroons and scoundrels.

8.
The Rewards of Virtue

I have spoken of the difficulties confronting an intelligent and honourable man who aspires to public office under this system. If he succeeds, it is only by a suspension of natural laws, and his success is seldom more than transient: his first term is commonly his last. And if, favoured by luck again, he goes on, it is only in the face of opposition of an almost incredible bitterness. The case of the Senator I have just mentioned is aptly in point. He is a man of obvious ability and integrity, but in his last campaign in Missouri he was opposed by a combination of all the parties and all their factions, with the waspish ghost of the late Dr. Wilson hanging over the battlefield. It was only his own amazing talents as a popular orator, aided by the post-war *Katzenjammer*[1] and a local delight in vigorous, rough-and-ready-fighters, that overcame the tremendous odds against him. In most other American States he would have been defeated easily; in many of them his defeat would have been overwhelming. Only in the newer States and in the border States have such men any chance at all. Where party fidelity has run strong for years they are barred from public life completely. No Senator of any genuine dignity and ability could come out of the Georgia of to-day, and none could come out of the Vermont. Such States must be content with party hacks, and the country as a whole must submit to their depressing imbecilities and ignoble contortions. All of them are men who have trimmed and fawned. All of them are forbidden a frank and competent discussion of most of the principal issues facing the nation.

But there is something yet worse, and that is the assumption of his cowardice and venality that lies upon even the most honourable man, brought into public office by a miracle. The mob is quite unable to grasp the concept of honour, and that incapacity is naturally shared by the vast majority of politicians. Thus the acts of a public man of genuine rectitude are almost always ascribed, under democracy, to sordid and degrading motives, *i.e.*, to the sort of motives that would animate his more orthodox colleagues if they were capable of his acts. I believe that the fact is more potent in keeping decent men out of public life in the United States than even the practical difficulties that I have rehearsed, and that it is mainly responsible for the astounding timorousness of our politics. Its effects were brilliantly displayed during the final stages of the battle over the Eighteenth Amendment. The Prohibitionist leaders, being mainly men of wide experience in playing upon the prejudices and emotions of the mob, developed a technique of terrorization that was almost irresistible. The moment a politician ventured to speak against them he was accused of the grossest baseness. It was whispered that he was a secret drunkard and eager to safeguard his tipple;

it was covertly hinted that he was in the pay of the Whiskey Ring,[2] the Beer Trust,[3] or some other such bugaboo. The event showed that the shoe was actually on the other foot—that many of the principal supporters of Prohibition were on the pay-roll of the Anti-Saloon League, and that judges, attorneys-general and other high officers of justice afterward joined them there. But the accusations served their purpose. The plain people, unable to imagine a man entering public life with any other motive than that which would have moved them themselves if they had been in his boots—that is to say, unable to imagine any other motive save a yearning for private advantage—reacted to the charges as if they had been proved, and so more than one man of relatively high decency, as decency goes in American life, was driven out of office. Upon those who escaped the lesson was not lost. It was five or six years before any considerable faction of politicians mustered up courage enough to defy the Prohibitionists, and even then what animated them was not any positive access of resolution but simply the fact that the Anti-Saloon League was obviously far gone in corruption,[4] with some of its chief agents in revolt against its methods, and others in prison for grave crimes and misdemeanours.

I am, myself, not cursed with the itch for public office, but I have been engaged for years in the discussion of public questions, and so I may be forgiven, I hope, for intruding my own experience here. That experience may be described briefly: there has never been a time when, attacking this or that current theory, I have not been accused of being in the pay of its interested opponents, and I believe that there has never been a time when this accusation was not generally believed. Years ago, when the Prohibitionists were first coming to power, they charged me with taking money from the brewers and distillers, and to-day they charge me with some sort of corrupt arrangement with the bootleggers, despite the plain fact that the latter are not their opponents at all, but their allies. The former accusation seemed so plausible to most Americans that even the brewers finally gave it credit: they actually offered to put me on their pay-roll, and were vastly surprised when I declined. It was simply impossible for them, as low-caste Americans, to imagine a man attempting to discharge a public duty disinterestedly; they believed that I had to be paid, as their rapidly dwindling *bloc* of Congressmen had to be paid. So in all other directions. When, fifteen or twenty years ago,[5] I began exposing the quackeries of osteopaths, chiropractors and other such frauds, they resorted instantly to the device of accusing me of taking a retainer from the mythical Medical Trust, *i.e.*, from such men as the Mayo brothers,[6] Dr. George Crile,[7] and the faculty of the Johns Hopkins.[8] Later on, venturing to denounce the nefarious political activity of the Methodist Church, and of its ally, the Ku Klux Klan, I was accused by spokesmen for the former of receiving bribes from the Vatican. The comstocks went even further. When I protested against their sinister and dishonest censorship of literature, they charged me publicly with being engaged in the circulation of pornography, and actually made a vain and ill-starred attempt to railroad me to jail on that charge.[9]

The point is that such accusations are generally believed, especially when they are leveled at a candidate for office. The average American knows what he would do in like case, and he believes quite naturally that every other man is willing and eager to do the same. At the start of my bout with the comstocks, just mentioned, many American newspapers assumed as a matter of course that I was guilty as charged, and some of them, having said so, were forced into elaborate explanations afterward to purge themselves of libel. Of the rest, most concluded that the whole combat was a sham battle, provoked on my own motion to give me what they regarded as profitable publicity. When I speak of newspapers, of course, I speak of concrete men, their editors.

These editors, under democracy, constitute an extremely powerful class. Their very lack of sound knowledge and genuine intelligence gives them a special fitness for influencing the mob, and it is augmented by their happy obtuseness to notions of honour. Their daily toil consists in part of praising men and ideas that are obviously fraudulent, and in part of denouncing men and ideas that are respected by their betters. The typical American editor, save in a few of the larger towns, may be described succinctly as one who has written a million words in favour of Coolidge and half a million against Darwin. He is, like the politician, an adept trimmer and flatterer. His job is far more to him than his self-respect. It must be plain that the influence of such men upon public affairs is generally evil—that their weight is almost always thrown against the public man of dignity and courage—that such a public man cannot hope to be understood by them, or to get any useful support from them. Even when they are friendly they are apt to be so for preposterous and embarrassing reasons. Thus they give their aid to the sublime democratic process of eliminating all sense and decency from public life. Coming out of the mob, they voice the ideas of the mob. The first of those ideas is that a fraud is somehow charming and reassuring—in the common phrase, that he is a regular fellow. The second is that an honest and candid man is dangerous—or, perhaps more accurately, that there is no such animal.

The newspaper editor who rises above this level encounters the same incredulous hostility from his fellows and his public that is encountered by the superior politician, cast into public life by accident. If he is not dismissed at once as what is now called a Bolshevik, *i.e.*, one harbouring an occult and unintelligible yearning to put down the Republic and pull God off His throne, he is assumed to be engaged in some nefarious scheme of personal aggrandizement. I point, as examples, to the cases of Fremont Older,[10] of San Francisco, and Julian Harris,[11] of

Columbus, Ga., two honest, able and courageous men, and both opposed by the vast majority of their colleagues. The democratic process, indeed, is furiously inimical to all honourable motives. It favours the man who is without them, and it puts heavy burdens upon the man who has them. Going further, it is even opposed to mere competence. The public servant who masters his job gains nothing thereby. His natural impatience with the incapacity and slacking of his fellows makes them his implacable enemies, and he is viewed with suspicion by the great mass of democrats. But here I enter upon a subject already discussed at length by a competent French critic, the late Emile Faguet,[12] of the French Academy, who gave a whole book to it, translated into English as "The Cult of Incompetence." Under democracy, says Faguet, the business of law-making becomes a series of panics—government by orgy and orgasm. And the public service becomes a mere refuge for prehensile morons—get yours, and run.

9.
Footnote on Lame Ducks

Faguet makes no mention of one of the curious and unpleasant by-products of democracy, of great potency for evil in both England and the United States: perhaps, for some unknown reason, it is less a nuisance in France. I allude to the sinister activity of professional politicians who, in the eternal struggle for office and its rewards, have suffered crushing defeats, and are full of rage and bitterness. All politics, under democracy. resolves itself into a series of dynastic questions: the objective is always the job, not the principle. The defeated candidate commonly takes his failure very badly, for it leaves him stripped bare. In most cases his fellow professionals take pity on him and put him into some more or less gaudy appointive office, to preserve his livelihood and save his face: the Federal commissions that harass the land are full of such lame ducks, and they are not unknown on the Federal bench. But now and then there appears one whose wounds are too painful to be assuaged by such devices, or for whom no suitable office can be found. This majestic victim not infrequently seeks surcease by a sort of running amok. That is to say, he turns what remains of his influence with the mob into a weapon against the nation as a whole, and becomes a chronic maker of trouble. The names of Burr, Clay, Calhoun, Douglas, Blaine, Greeley, Frémont, Roosevelt and Bryan[1] will occur to every attentive student of American history. There have been many similar warlocks on lower levels; they are familiar in the politics of every American county.

Clay, like Bryan after him, was three times a candidate for the Presidency. Defeated in 1824, 1832 and 1840,[2] he turned his back upon democracy, and became the first public agent and attorney for what are now called the Interests. When he died he was the darling of the Mellons, Morgans and Charlie Schwabs[3] of his time. He believed in centralization and in the blessings of a protective tariff. These blessings the American people still enjoy. Calhoun, deprived of the golden plum by an unappreciative country, went even further. He seems to have come to the conclusion that its crime made it deserve capital punishment. At all events, he threw his strength into the plan to break up the Union. The doctrine of Nullification owed more to him than it owed to any other politician, and after 1832, when his hopes of getting into the White House were finally extinguished, he devoted himself whole-heartedly to preparing the way for the Civil War. He was more to blame for that war, in all probability, than any other man. But if he had succeeded Jackson[4] the chances are that he would have sung a far less bellicose tune. The case of Burr is so plain that it has even got into the school history-books. If he had beaten Jefferson in 1800 there would have been no duel with Hamilton, no conspiracy with Blennerhassett,[5] no trial for treason, and no long exile and venomous repining. Burr was an able man, as politicians go under democracy, and the young Republic stood in great need of his peculiar talents. But his failure to succeed Adams made a misanthrope of him, and his misanthropy was vented upon his country, and more than once brought it to the verge of disaster.

There have been others like him in our own time: Blaine, Frémont, Hancock,[6] Roosevelt, Bryan. If Blaine had been elected in 1876 he would have ceased to wave the bloody shirt;[7] as it was, he was still waving it, recklessly and obscenely, in 1884. No man laboured more assiduously to keep alive the hatreds flowing out of the Civil War; his whole life was poisoned by his failure to reach the White House, and his dreadful cramps and rages led him into a long succession of obviously anti-social acts. Roosevelt went the same route. His débâcle in 1912[8] converted him into a sort of political killer, and until the end of his life he was constantly on the warpath, looking for heads to crack. The outbreak of the World War in 1914 brought him great embarrassment, for he had been the most ardent American exponent, for years past, of what was then generally regarded as the German scheme of things.[9] For a few weeks he was irresolute, and seemed likely to stick to his guns. But then, perceiving a chance to annoy and damage his successful enemy, Wilson, he swallowed the convictions of a lifetime, and took the other side. That his ensuing uproars had evil effects must he manifest. Regardless of the consequences, either at home or abroad, he kept on arousing the mob against Wilson, and in the end he helped more than any other man to force the United States into the war. His aim, it quickly appeared, was to turn the situation to his own advantage: he made desperate and shameless efforts to get a high military command at the front—a post for which he was plainly unfitted. When Wilson, still smarting from his attack, vetoed this scheme, he broke into fresh rages, and the rest of his life was more pathological than political. The fruits of his reckless demagogy are still with us.

Bryan was even worse. His third defeat, in 1908, convinced even so vain a fellow that the White House was beyond his reach, and so he consecrated himself to reprisals upon those who had kept him out of it. He saw very clearly who they were: the more intelligent minority of his countrymen. It was their unanimous opposition that had thrice thrown the balance against him. Well, he would now make them infamous. He would raise the mob, which still admired him, against everything they regarded as sound sense and intellectual decency. He would post them as sworn foes to all true virtue and true religion, and try, if possible, to put them down by law. There ensued his frenzied campaign against the teaching of evolution—perhaps the most gross attack upon human dignity and decorum ever made by a politician, even under democracy, in modern times. Those who regarded him, in his last years, as a mere religious fanatic were far in error. It was not fanaticism that moved him, but hatred. He was an ambulent boil, as anyone could see who encountered him face to face. His theological ideas were actually very vague; he was quite unable to defend them competently under Clarence Darrow's[10] cross-examination. What moved him was simply his colossal lust for revenge upon those he held to be responsible for his downfall as a politician. He wanted to hurt them, proscribe them; if possible, destroy them. To that end he was willing to sacrifice everything else, including the public tranquillity and the whole system of public education. He passed out of life at last at a temperature of 110 degrees, his eyes rolling horribly toward 1600 Pennsylvania avenue, N.W.[11] and its leaky copper roof. In the suffering South his fever lives after him. The damage he did was greater than that done by Sherman's army.[12]

Countries under the hoof of despotism escape such lamentable exhibitions of human frailly. Unsuccessful aspirants for the crown are either butchered out of hand or exiled to Paris, where tertiary lues[13] quickly disposes of them. The Crown Prince, of course, has his secret thoughts, and no doubt they are sometimes homicidal, but he is forced by etiquette to keep them to himself, and so the people are not annoyed and injured by them. He cannot go about praying publicly that the King, his father, come down with endocarditis, nor can he denounce the old gentleman as an idiot and advocate his confinement in a *maison de santé.*[14] Everyone, of course, knows what his hopes and yearnings are, but no one has to listen to them. If he voices them at all it is only to friendly and discreet members of the diplomatic corps and to the ladies of the half and quarter worlds.[15] Under democracy, they are bellowed from every stump.

III
Democracy and Liberty

1.
The Will to Peace

Whenever the liberties of *Homo vulgaris*[1] are invaded and made a mock of in a gross and contemptuous manner, as happened, for example, in the United States during the reign of Wilson, Palmer, Burleson[2] and company, there are always observers who marvel that he bears the outrage with so little murmuring. Such observers only display their unfamiliarity with the elements of democratic science. The truth is that the common man's love of liberty, like his love of sense, justice and truth, is almost wholly imaginary. As I have argued, he is not actually happy when free; he is uncomfortable, a bit alarmed, and intolerably lonely. He longs for the warm, reassuring smell of the herd, and is willing to take the herdsman with it. Liberty is not a thing for such as he. He cannot enjoy it rationally himself, and he can think of it in others only as something to be taken away from them. It is, when it becomes a reality, the exclusive possession of a small and disreputable minority of men, like knowledge, courage and honour. A special sort of man is needed to understand it, nay, to stand it—and he is inevitably an outlaw in democratic societies. The average man doesn't want to be free. He simply wants to be safe.

Nietzsche,[3] with his usual clarity of vision, saw the point clearly. Liberty, he used to say, was something that, to the general, was too cold to be borne. Nevertheless, he apparently believed that there was an unnatural, drug-store sort of yearning for it in *all* men, and so he changed Schopenhauer's[4] will-to-live into a will-to-power. *i. e.*, a will-to-free-function. Here he went too far, and in the wrong direction: he should have made it, on the lower levels, a will-to-peace. What the common man longs for in this world, before and above all his other longings, is the simplest and most ignominious sort of peace—the peace of a trusty in a well-managed penitentiary. He is willing to sacrifice everything else to it. He puts it above his dignity and he puts it above his pride. Above all, he puts it above his liberty. The fact, perhaps, explains his veneration for policemen, in all the forms they take—his belief that there is a mysterious sanctity in law, however absurd it may be in fact. A policeman is a charlatan who offers, in return for obedience, to protect him *(a)* from his superiors, *(b)* from his equals, and *(c)* from himself. This last service, under democracy, is commonly the most esteemed of them all. In the United States, at least theoretically, it is the only thing that keeps ice-wagon drivers, Y. M. C. A. secretaries, insurance collectors and other such human camels from smoking opium, ruining themselves in the night clubs, and going to Palm Beach with Follies girls. It is a democratic invention.

Here, though the common man is deceived, he starts from a sound premiss: to wit, that liberty is something too hot for his hands—or, as Nietzsche put it, too cold for his spine. Worse, he sees in it something that is a weapon against him in the hands of his enemy, the man of superior kidney. Be true to your nature, and follow its teachings: this Emersonian counsel,[5] it must be manifest, offers an embarrassing support to every variety of the *droit de seigneur.*[6] The history of democracy is a history of efforts to force successive minorities to be untrue to their nature. Democracy, in fact, stands in greater peril of the free spirit than any sort of despotism ever heard of. The despot, at least, is always safe in one respect: his own belief in himself cannot he shaken. But democracies may be demoralized and run amok, and so they are in vast dread of heresy, as a Sunday-school superintendent is in dread of scarlet women, light wines and beer, and the unreadable works of Charles Darwin. It would be unimaginable for a democracy to submit serenely to such gross dissents as Frederick the Great not only permitted, but even encouraged. Once the mob is on the loose, there is no holding it. So the subversive minority must be reduced to impotence; the heretic must be put down.

If, as they say, one of the main purposes of all civilized government is to preserve and augment the liberty of the individual, then surely democracy accomplishes it less efficiently than any other form. Is the individual worth thinking of at all? Then the superior individual is worth more thought than his inferiors. But it is precisely the superior individual who is the chief victim of the democratic process. It not only tries to regulate his acts; it also tries to delimit his thoughts; it is constantly inventing new forms of the old crime of imagining the King's death. The Roman *lex de majestate*[7] was put upon the books, not by an emperor, nor even by a consul, but by Saturninus,[8] a tribune of the people. Its aim was to protect the state against aristocrats, *i.e.*, against free spirits, each holding himself answerable only to his own notions. The aim of democracy is to break all such free spirits to the common harness. It tries to iron them out, to pump them dry of self-respect, to make docile John Does of them. The measure of its success is the extent to which such men are brought down, and made common. The measure of civilization is the extent to which they resist and survive. Thus the only sort of liberty that is real under democracy is the liberty of the have-nots to destroy the liberty of the haves.

This liberty is supposed, in some occult way, to enhance human dignity. Perhaps, in one of its aspects, it actually does. The have-not gains something valuable when he acquires the delusion that he is the equal of his betters. It may not be true—but even a delusion, if it augments the dignity of man, is something. Certain apparent realities grow out of it: the peasant no longer pulls his forelock[9] when he meets the baron, he is free to sue and be sued, he may denounce Huxley[10] as a quack. But the thing, alas, works both ways. As one pan of the scale goes up, the other comes down. If democracy really loves the dignity of man, then it kills the thing it loves. Where it prevails, not even the King can be dignified in any rational sense: he becomes Harding, jabbering of normalcy,[11] or Coolidge, communing with his preposterous *Tabakparlement*[12] around the stove. Nor the Pope: he becomes a Methodist bishop in a natty business-suit, and with a toothbrush moustache. Nor the Generalissimo: he becomes Pershing,[13] haranguing Rotary, and slapping the backs of his fellow Elks.

2.
The Democrat as Moralist

Liberty gone, there remains the majestic phenomenon of democratic law. A glance at it is sufficient to show the identity of democracy and Puritanism. The two, indeed, are but different facets of the same gem. In the psyche they are one. For both get their primal essence out of the inferior man's fear and hatred of his betters, born of his observation that, for all his fine theories, they are stronger and of more courage then he is, and that as they go through this dreadful world they have a far better time. Thus envy comes in; if you overlook it you will never understand democracy, and you will never understand Puritanism. It is not, of course, a speciality of democratic man. It is the common possession of all men of the ignoble and incompetent sort, at all times and everywhere. But it is only under democracy that it is liberated; it is only under democracy that it becomes the philosophy of the state. What the human race owes to the old autocracies, and how little, in these democratic days, it is disposed to remember the debt! Their service, perhaps, was a by-product of a purpose far afield, but it was a service none the less: they held the green fury of the mob in check, and so set free the spirit of superior man. Their collapse under Flavius Honorius[1] left Europe in chaos for four hundred years. Their revival under Charlemagne[2] made the Renaissance possible, and the modern age. What the thing was that they kept from the throat of civilization has been shown more than once in these later days, by the failure of their enfeebled successors. I point to the only too obvious examples of the French and Russian Revolutions. The instant such a catastrophe liberates the mob, it begins a war to the death upon superiority of every kind—not only upon the kind that naturally attaches to autocracy, but even upon the kind that stands in opposition to it. The day after a successful revolution is a blue day for the late autocrat, but it is also a blue day for every other superior man. The murder of Lavoisier[3] was a phenomenon quite as significant as the murder of Louis XVI.[4] We need no scientists in France, shouted MM. of the Revolutionary Tribunal. Wat Tyler,[5] four centuries before, reduced it to an even greater frankness and simplicity: he hanged every man who confessed to being able to read and write.

Democracy, as a political scheme, may be defined as a device for releasing this hatred born of envy, and for giving it the force and dignity of law. Tyler, in the end, was dispatched by Walworth; under democracy he becomes almost the ideal Good Man.[6] It is very difficult to disentangle the political ideas of this anthropoid Good Man from his theological ideas: they constantly overlap and coalesce, and the democratic state, despite the contrary example of France, almost always shows a strong tendency to be also a Puritan state. Puritan legislation, especially in the field of public law, is a thing of many grandiose pretensions and a few simple and ignoble realities. The Puritan, discussing it voluptuously, always tries to convince himself (and the rest of us) that it is grounded upon altruistic and evangelical motives—that its aim is to work the other fellow's benefit against the other fellow's will. Such is the theory behind Prohibition, comstockery,[7] vice crusading, and all its other familiar devices of oppression. That theory, of course, is false. The Puritan's actual motives are *(a)* to punish the other fellow for having a better time in the world, and *(b)* to bring the other fellow down to his own unhappy level. Such are his punitive and remedial purposes. Primarily, he is against every human act that he is incapable of himself—safely. The adverb tells the whole story. The Puritan is surely no ascetic. Even in the great days of the New England theocracy it was impossible to restrain his libidinousness: his eyes rolled sideways at buxom wenches quite as often as they rolled upward to God. But he is incapable of sexual experience upon what may be called a civilized plane; it is impossible for him to manage the thing as a romantic adventure; in his hands it reduces itself to the terms of the barnyard. Hence the Mann Act. So with dalliance with the grape. He can have experience of it only as a furtive transaction behind the door, with a dreadful headache to follow. Hence Prohibition. So, again, with the joys that come out of the fine arts. Looking at a picture, he sees only the model's pudenda. Reading a book, he misses the ordeals and exaltations of the spirit, and remembers only the natural functions. Hence comstockery.

His delight in his own rectitude is grounded upon a facile assumption that it is difficult to maintain—that the other fellow, being deficient in God's grace, is incapable of it. So he venerates himself, in the moral department, as an artist of unusual talents, a virtuoso of virtue. His error consists in mistaking a weakness for a merit, an inferiority for a superiority. It is not actually a sign of spiritual eminence to be moral in the Puritan sense: it is simply a sign of docility, of lack of enterprise and originality, of cowardice. The Puritan, once his mainly imaginary triumphs over the flesh and the devil are forgotten, always turns out to be a poor stick of a man—in brief, a natural democrat. His triumphs in the field of government are as illusory as his triumphs as metaphysician and artist. No Puritan has ever painted a picture worth looking at, or written a symphony worth hearing; or a poem worth reading—and I am not forgetting John Milton,[8] who was not a Puritan at all, but a libertarian, which is the exact opposite. The whole Puritan literature is comprised in "The Pilgrim's Progress."[9] Even in the department wherein the Puritan is most proud of himself, *i.e.,* that of moral legislation, he has done only second and third rate work. His fine schemes for bringing his betters down to his own depressing level always turn out badly. In the whole history of human lawmaking there is no record of a failure worse than that of Prohibition in the United States. Since the first uprising of the lower orders, the modern age has seen but one genuinely valuable contribution to moral legislation: I allude, of course, to the Code Napoléon.[10] It was concocted by a committee of violent anti-Puritans, and in the full tide of a bitter reaction against democracy.

If democracy had not lain implicit in Puritanism, Puritanism would have had to invent it. Each is necessary to the other. Democracy provides the machinery that Puritanism needs for the quick and ruthless execution of its preposterous inventions. Facing autocracy, it faces insuperable difficulties, for its spokesmen can convince the King only in case he is crazy, and even when he is crazy he is commonly restrained by his ministers. But the mob is easy to convince, for what Puritanism has to say to it is mainly what it already believes: its politics is based upon the same brutal envies and quaking fears that lie under the Puritan ethic. Moreover, the political machinery through which it functions provides a ready means of translating such envies and fears into action. There is need only to sound the alarm and take a vote: the debate is over the moment the majority has spoken. The fact explains the ferocious haste with which, in democratic countries, even the most strange and dubious legislative experiments are launched. Haste is necessary, lest even the mob be shaken by sober second thought. And haste is easy, for the appeal to the majority is officially the last appeal of all, and when it has been made there is the best of excuses for cutting off debate. I have described the precise process in a previous section. Fanatics inflame the mob, and thereby alarm the scoundrels set up to make laws in its name. The scoundrels precipitately do the rest. The Fathers were not unaware of this danger in the democratic scheme.[11] They sought to counteract it by establishing upper chambers, removed by at least one degree from the mob's hot rages. Their precaution has been turned to naught by depriving the upper chambers of that prophylactic remoteness, and exposing them to the direct and unmitigated blast.

It must be plain that this process of lawmaking by orgy, with fanatics supplying the motive-power and unconscionable knaves steering the machine, is bound to fill the statute-books with enactments that have no rational use or value save that of serving as instruments of psychopathological persecution and private revenge. This is found to be the case, in fact, in almost every American State. The grotesque anti-syndicalist laws of California, the anti-evolution laws of Tennessee and Mississippi, and the acts for the enforcement of Prohibition in Ohio and Indiana are typical.[12] They involve gross invasions of the most elementary rights of the free citizen, but they are popular with the mob because they have a virtuous smack and provide it with an endless succession of barbarous but thrilling shows. Their chosen victims are men the mob naturally envies and hates—men of unusual intelligence and enterprise, men who regard their constitutional liberties seriously and are willing to go to some risk and expense to defend them. Such men are inevitably unpopular under democracy, for their qualities are qualities that the mob wholly lacks, and is uneasily conscious of lacking: it thus delights in seeing them exposed to slander and oppression, and railroaded to prison. There is always a district attorney at hand to launch the prosecution, for district attorneys are invariably men who aspire to higher office, and no more facile way to it is to be found than by assaulting and destroying a man above the general. As I have shown, many an American Congressman comes to Washington from a district attorney's office: you may be sure that he is seldom promoted because he has been jealous of the liberties of the citizen. Many a judge reaches the bench by the same route—and thereafter benignantly helps along his successors. The whole criminal law in America thus acquires a flavour of fraud. It is constantly embellished and reinforced by fanatics who have discovered how easy it is to hurl missiles at their enemies and opponents from behind ranks of policemen. It is executed by law officers whose private prosperity runs in direct ratio to their reckless ferocity. And the business is applauded by morons whose chief delight lies in seeing their betters manhandled and humiliated. Even the ordinary criminal law is so carried out—that is, when the accused happens to be conspicuous enough to make it worthwhile. Every district attorney in America goes to his knees every night to ask God to deliver a Thaw[13] or a Fatty Arbuckle[14] into his hands.

In the criminal courts a rich man not only enjoys none of the advantages that Liberals and other defenders of democracy constantly talk of; he is under very real and very heavy burdens. The defence that Thaw offered in the White case would have got a taxi-driver acquitted in five minutes. And had Arbuckle been a waiter, no district attorney in the land would have dreamed of putting him on trial for first-degree murder.

For such foul and pestiferous proceedings, of course, moral excuses are always offered. The district attorney is an altruist whose one dream is Law Enforcement; he cannot be terrified by the power of money; he is the spokesman of the virtuous masses against the godless and abominable classes. The same buncombe issues from the Prohibitionists, comstocks, hunters of Bolshevists, and other such frauds. Its hollowness is constantly revealed. The Prohibitionists, when they foisted their brummagem cure-all upon the country under cover of the war hysteria,[15] gave out that their advocacy of it was based upon a Christian yearning to abate drunkenness, and so abolish crime, poverty and disease. They preached a millennium, and no doubt convinced hundreds of thousands of naïve and sentimental persons, not themselves Puritans, nor even democrats. That millennium, as everyone knows, has failed to come in. Not only are crime, poverty and disease undiminished, but drunkenness itself, if the police statistics are to be believed, has greatly increased. The land rocks with the scandal. Prohibition has made the use of alcohol devilish and even fashionable, and so vastly augmented the number of users. The young of both sexes, mainly innocent of the cup under license, now take to it almost unanimously. In brief, Prohibition has not only failed to work the benefits that its proponents promised in 1917; it has brought in so many new evils that even the mob has turned against it. But do the Prohibitionists admit the fact frankly, and repudiate their original nonsense? They do not. On the contrary, they keep on demanding more and worse enforcement statutes—that is to say, more and worse devices for harassing and persecuting their opponents. The more obvious the failure becomes, the more shamelessly they exhibit their genuine motives. In plain words, what moves them is the psychological aberration called sadism. They lust to inflict inconvenience, discomfort, and, whenever possible, disgrace upon the persons they hate—which is to say, upon everyone who is free from their barbarous theological superstitions, and is having a better time in the world than they are. They cannot stop the use of alcohol, nor even appreciably diminish it, but they *can* badger and annoy everyone who seeks to use it decently, and they *can* fill the jails with men taken for purely artificial offences, and they *can* get satisfaction thereby for the Puritan yearning to browbeat and injure, to torture and terrorize, to punish and humiliate all who show any sign of being happy. And all this they can do with a safe line of policemen and judges in front of them; always they can do it without personal risk.

It is this freedom from personal risk that is the secret of the Prohibitionists' continued frenzy, despite the complete collapse of Prohibition itself. They know very well that the American mob, far from being lawless, is actually excessively tolerant of written laws and judicial fiats, however plainly they violate the fundamental rights of free men, and they know that this tolerance is sufficient to protect them from what, in more liberal and enlightened countries, would be the natural consequences of their anti-social activity. If they had to meet their victims face to face, there would be a different story to tell. But, like their brethren, the comstocks and the professional patriots, they seldom encounter this embarrassment. Instead, they turn the officers of the law to the uses of their mania. More, they reinforce the officers of the law with an army of bravos sworn to take their orders and do their bidding—the army of so-called Prohibition enforcement officers, mainly made up of professional criminals. Thus, under democracy, the normal, well-behaved, decent citizen—the Forgotten Man of the late William Graham Sumner[16]—is beset from all sides, and every year sees an augmentation of his woes. In order to satisfy the envy and hatred of his inferiors and the blood lust of a pack of irresponsible and unconscionable fanatics, few of them of any dignity as citizens or as men and many of them obviously hypocritical and corrupt, this decent citizen is converted into a criminal for performing acts that are natural to men of his class everywhere, and police and courts are degraded to the abhorrent office of punishing him for them.

Certainly it should not be surprising that such degrading work has greatly diminished the authority of both—that Prohibition has made the courts disreputable and increased general crime. A judge who jails a well-disposed and inoffensive citizen for violating an unjust and dishonest law may be defended plausibly, perhaps, by legal casuistry, but it is very hard to make out a case for him as a self-respecting man. Like the ordinary politician, he puts his job above his professional dignity and his common decency. More than one judge, unable to square such loathsome duties with his private notions of honor, has stepped down from the bench, and left the business to a successor who was more a lawyer and less a man.

3.
Where Puritanism Fails

Under the pressure of fanaticism, and with the mob complacently applauding the show, democratic law tends more and more to be grounded upon the maxim that every citizen is, by nature, a traitor, a libertine, and a scoundrel. In order to dissuade him from his evil-doing the police power is extended until it surpasses anything ever heard of in the oriental monarchies of antiquity. In many American States—for example, California and Pennsylvania[1]—it is almost a literal fact that the citizen has no rights that the police are bound to respect. These awful powers, of course, are not exercised against *all* citizens. The man of influence with the reigning politicians, the supporter of the prevailing delusions, and the adept hypocrite—these are seldom molested. But the man who finds himself in an unpopular minority is at the mercy of the *Polizei*,[2] and the easiest way to get into such a minority is to speak out boldly for the Bill of Rights.[3] Men have been clubbed and jailed in Pennsylvania for merely mentioning it; scores have been jailed for protesting publicly against its violation. Here the attack was at least frank, and, to that extent, honest; more often it is made disingenuously, and to the tune of pious snuffling. First an unpopular man is singled out for persecution, and then a diligent search is made, with the police and prosecuting officers and even the courts co-operating, for a law that he can be accused of breaking. The enormous multiplicity of sumptuary and inquisitorial statutes makes this quest easy. The prisoner begins his progress through the mill of justice under a vague accusation of disorderly conduct or disturbing the peace; he ends charged with crimes that carry staggering penalties. There are statutes in many States, notably California, that explore his mind, and lay him by the heels for merely thinking unpopular thoughts.[4] Once he is accused of such heresy, the subsequent proceedings take on the character of a lynching. His constitutional rights are swept away as of no validity, and all the ancient rules of the Common Law—for example, those against double jeopardy and hearsay—are suspended in order to fetch him. Many of the newer statutes actually suspend these safeguards formally, and though they are to that extent plainly unconstitutional, the higher courts have not interfered with their execution. The Volstead Act, for instance, destroys the constitutional right to a jury trial, and in its administration the constitutional prohibition of unreasonable searches and seizures and the rule against double jeopardy are habitually violated. But no protest comes save from specialists in liberty, most of whom are so busy keeping out of jail themselves that their caveats are feeble and ineffective. The mob is always in favour of the prosecution, for the prosecution is giving the show. In the face of its applause, very few American judges have the courage to enforce the Constitutional guarantees—and still fewer prosecuting attorneys. As I have said, a prosecuting attorney's success depends very largely upon his ferocity. American practice permits him an extravagance of attack that would land him in jail, and perhaps even in a lunatic asylum, in any other country, and the more passionately he indulges in it the more certain becomes his promotion to higher office, including the judicial. Perhaps a half of all American judges, at some time or other, have been prosecuting officers. They carry to the bench the habits of mind acquired on the other side of the bar; they seem to be generally convinced that any man accused of crime is *ipso facto*[5] guilty, and that if he is known to harbour political heresies he is guilty of a sort of blasphemy when he mentions his constitutional rights.

This doctrine that a man who stands in contempt of the prevailing idealogy has no rights under the law is so thoroughly democratic that in the United States it is seldom questioned save by romantic fanatics, robbed of their wits by an uncritical reading of the Fathers. It not only goes unchallenged otherwise; it is openly stated and defended, and by high authorities. I point, for example, to the Right Rev. Luther B. Wilson, who, as a bishop of the Methodist Episcopal Church, occupies an office that is both ecclesiastical and political, and is of dignity and puissance in both fields. Some time ago this Wilson was invited to preach in the Cathedral of St. John the Divine in New York—a delicate acknowledgment of his importance by his rival prelate of the Anglican Church, Monsignor Manning. His sermon, in brief, was a passionate plea for the putting down of heresy, law or no law, Constitution or no Constitution. "Atheism," he declared, "is not only folly, but to the state a traitor. It does not deserve a place and should not be defended by any specious claim for immunity under the constitutional guaranties of the right of free speech."[6] This bloodthirsty and astounding dictum, though it came from a Christian ecclesiastic of a rank higher than that attained by Christ Himself, seemed so natural that it attracted no notice whatever. Not a single New York newspaper challenged it; even the Liberal weeklies let it pass as too obvious for cavil.

A week or so later it was printed with approbation in all the Methodist denominational organs, and since then many other bishops of that sect have ratified it. The same doctrine is frequently stated plainly by high legal officers, especially when a man accused of political heresy is on trial—usually, of course, for an alleged infraction of the ordinary law. As I have said in a previous chapter, it was applied to atheists, exactly as Bishop Wilson applied it, during the celebrated Scopes trial at Dayton, Tenn. Arthur Garfield Hays,[7] defending Scopes, arose at one point in the proceedings to protest that they were going beyond the bounds of due process—that his client was not getting a fair and impartial trial within the meaning of the Constitution. At once the prosecuting attorney general, Stewart,[8] answered candidly that an atheist had no right to a fair trial in Tennessee, and the judge on the bench, the learned Raulston,[9] approved with a nod. Hays, who is a Liberal, was so overcome that he sank in his place with a horrified gurgle, but the Tennesseans in the courtroom saw nothing strange in Stewart's reply. They knew very well that, in all the States South of the Potomac, save only Louisiana, Catholics, Negroes and all the persons unable to speak the local dialects fluently shared the disability of atheists. And if they were learned in American law, they knew that anti-Catholics faced the same disability in Massachusetts, like anti-Semites in New York, and that in every State there were classes similarly proscribed. I do not here allude to the natural difficulty that every man of notoriously heterodox ideas must encounter every time he faces a jury, which is to say, twelve men of limited information and intelligence, chosen precisely because of their lack of intellectual resilience.[10] I am speaking of the hostility he must look for in prosecuting officers and judges, and in the newspapers that sit in judgment upon them and largely determine their fortunes. I am speaking of what has come to be a settled practice in American criminal law.

It is difficult, indeed, for democracy to reconcile itself to what may be called common decency. By this common decency I mean the habit, in the individual, of viewing with tolerance and charity the acts and ideas of other individuals—the habit which makes a man a reliable friend, a generous opponent, and a good citizen. The democrat, despite his strong opinion to the contrary, is seldom a good citizen. In that sense, as in most others, he falls distressfully short. His eagerness to bring all his fellow-citizens, and especially all those who are superior to him, into accord with his own dull and docile way of thinking, and to force it upon them when they resist, leads him inevitably into acts of unfairness, oppression and dishonour which, if all men were alike guilty of them, would quickly break down that mutual trust and confidence upon which the very structure of civilized society rests. Where democratic man is so firmly in possession of his theoretical rights that resistance to him is hopeless, as it is in large areas of the United States, he actually produces this disaster. To live in a community so cursed is almost impossible to any man who does not accept the democratic epistemology and the Puritan ethic, which is to say, to any well-informed and self-respecting man. He is harassed in so many small ways, and with such depressing violence and lack of decency, that he is usually compelled to clear out. This fact, in large part, explains the cultural collapse of New England and the marked cultural backwardness of whole regions in the South and Middle West. A man of sound sense, born into the Tennessee hinterland, not only feels lonesome as he comes to maturity; he also feels unsafe. The morons surrounding him hate him, and if they can't lay him for mere heresy, they will wait their chance and lay him for burning barns, for poisoning wells, or for taking Russian gold.[11] So he departs.

This irreconcilable antagonism between democratic Puritanism and common decency is probably responsible for the uneasiness and unhappiness that are so marked in American life, despite the great material prosperity of the United States. Theoretically, the American people should be happier than any other; actually, they are probably the least happy in Christendom. The trouble with them is that they do not trust one another—and without mutual trust there can be no ease, and no genuine happiness. What avails it for a man to have money in the bank and a Ford in his garage if he knows that his neighbours on both sides are watching him through knotholes, and that the pastor of the tabernacle down the road is planning to have him sent to jail? The thing that makes life charming is not money, but the society of our fellow men, and the thing that draws us toward our fellow men is not admiration for their inner virtues, their hard striving to live according to the light that is in them, but admiration for their outer graces and decencies—in brief, confidence that they will always act generously and understandingly in their intercourse with us. We must trust men before we may enjoy them. Manifestly, it is impossible to put any such trust in a Puritan. With the best intentions in the world he cannot rid himself of the delusion that his duty to save us from our sins—*i. e.*, from the non-Puritanical acts that we delight in—is paramount to his duty to let us be happy in our own way. Thus he is unable to be tolerant, and with tolerance goes magnanimity. A Puritan cannot be magnanimous. He is constitutionally unable to grasp the notion that it is better to be decent than to be steadfast, or even than to be just. So with the democrat, who is simply a Puritan doubly damned. When the late Dr. Wilson, confronted by the case of poor old silly Debs,[12] decided instantly that Debs must remain in jail, he acted as a true democrat and a perfect Puritan. The impulse to be magnanimous, to forgive and forget, to be kindly and generous toward a misguided and harmless old man, was overcome by the harsh Puritan compulsion to observe the letter of the law at all costs. Every Puritan is a lawyer, and so is every democrat.

4.
Corruption Under Democracy

This moral compulsion of the Puritan and democrat, of course, is mainly bogus. When one has written off cruelty, envy and cowardice, one has accounted for nine-tenths of it. Certainly I need not argue at this late date that the *Ur*-Puritan of New England was by no means the vestal that his heirs and assigns think of when they praise him. He was not only a very carnal fellow, and given to lamentable transactions with loose women and fiery jugs; he was also a virtuoso of sharp practices, and to this day his feats in that department survive in fable. Nor is there any perceptible improvement in his successors. When a gang of real estate agents (*i. e.* rent sweaters), bond salesmen* and automobile dealers gets together to sob for Service, it takes no Freudian to surmise that someone is about to be swindled. The cult of Service,[1] indeed, is half a sop to conscience, and half a bait to catch conies. Its cultivation in the United States runs parallel with the most gorgeous development of imposture as a fine art that Christendom has ever seen. I speak of a fine art in the literal sense; in the form of advertising it enlists such talents as, under less pious civilizations, would be devoted to the confection of cathedrals, and even, perhaps, masses. A sixth of the Americano's income is rooked out of him by rogues who have at him officially, and in the name of the government; half the remainder goes to sharpers who prefer the greater risks and greater profits of private enterprise. All schemes to save him from such victimizations have failed in the past, and all of them, I believe, are bound to fail in the future; most of the more gaudy of them are simply devices to facilitate fresh victimizations. For democratic man, dreaming eternally of Utopias, is ever a prey to shibboleths, and those that fetch him in his politi-

*Correcting "salesman" in original text.

cal capacity are more than matched by those that fetch him in his role of private citizen. His normal and natural situation, held through all the vicissitudes of his brief history, has been that of one who, at great cost and effort, has sneaked home a jug of contraband whiskey, sworn to have issued out of a padlocked distillery, and then finds, on uncorking it, that it is a compound of pepper, prune juice and wood alcohol.[2] This, in a sentence, is the history of democracy. It is, in detail, the history of all such characteristically democratic masterpieces as Bryanism, Ku Kluxery, and the war to end war.[3] They are full of virtuous pretences, and they are unmitigated swindles.

All observers of democracy, from Tocqueville[4] to the Adams brothers[5] and Wilfrid Scawen Blunt,[6] have marveled at its corruptions on the political side, and speculated heavily as to the causes thereof. The fact was noted in the earliest days of the democratic movement, and Friedrich von Gentz,[7] who began life as an Anglomaniac, was using it as an argument against the parliamentary system so early as 1809. Gentz, who served Metternich[8] as the current Washington correspondents serve whatever dullard happens to be President, contended that the introduction of democracy on the Continent would bring in a reign of bribery, and thus destroy the integrity and authority of the state. The proofs that he was right were already piling up, in his day, in the United States. They were destined to be greatly reinforced when the Third Republic[9] got under way in France in 1870, and to be given impressive support when the German Republic[10] set up shop in 1918. In 1919, for the first time since the coronation of Henry the Fowler, a German Cabinet minister crossed the border between days, his loot under his arm. The historians, immersed in their closets, marvel that such things happen, and marvel even more that democracy takes them calmly, and even lightly. Somewhere in "The Education of Henry Adams" you will find an account of the gigantic peculations that went on during the second Grant[11] administration, and melancholy reflections upon the populace's philosophic acceptance of them as inevitable, and even natural. In our own time we have seen the English mob embrace and elevate to higher office the democratic statesmen caught in the Marconi scandal,[12] and the American mob condone almost automatically the herculean raids upon the Treasury that marked the Wilson administration,[13] and the less spectacular but even more deliberate thievings that went on under the martyred Harding.[14] In the latter case it turned upon the small body of specialists in rectitude who ventured to protest, and in the end they found themselves far more unpopular than the thieves.

Such phenomena, as I say, puzzle the more academic pathologists of democracy, but as for me, I only say that they seem to be in strict accord with God's invariable laws. Why should democracy rise against bribery? It is itself a form of wholesale bribery. In place of a government with a fixed purpose and a visible goal, it sets up a government that is a mere function of the mob's vagaries, and that maintains itself by constantly bargaining with those vagaries. Its security depends wholly upon providing satisfactory bribes for the prehensile minorities that constitute the mob, or that have managed to deceive and inflame the mob. One day the labour leaders—a government within the general government—must be bought with offices; the next day the dupes of these labour leaders must be bought with legislation, usually of a sort loading the ordinary scales of justice in their favour; the day after there must be something for the manufacturers, for the Methodists, for the Catholics, for the farmers. I have exhibited, in another work, the fact that this last class demands bribes pure and simple—that its yearnings for its own private advantage are never ameliorated by yearnings for the common good.[15] The whole process of government under democracy, as everyone knows, is a process of similar trading. The very head of the state, having no title to his office save that which lies in the popular will, is forced to haggle and bargain like the lowliest office-seeker. There has been no President of the United States since Washington who did not go into office with a long list of promises in his pocket, and nine-tenths of them have always been promises of private reward from the public store. It is surely not regarded as immoral, by the democratic ethic, to make and execute such promises, though statesmen of lofty pretensions, *e.g.*, Lincoln, sometimes deny having made them. What is reproached as immoral is making them, and then not keeping them. When the late Dr. Wilson made William Jennings Bryan his Secretary of State the act brought forth only tolerant smiles, though it was comparable to appointing a chiropractor Surgeon General of the Army—a feat which Dr. Harding, a few years later, escaped performing only by a hair. But if Wilson had forgotten his obligation to Bryan there would have been an outburst of moral indignation, even among Bryan's enemies, and the collapse of Wilson would have come long before it did. When he blew up at last it was not because, after promulgating his Fourteen Points,[16] he joined in swindling a helpless foe[17] at Versailles; it was because he tried, at Paris, to undo some of the consequences of that fraud by forcing the United States into the League of Nations.[18] A democratic state, indeed, is so firmly grounded upon cheats and humbugs of all sorts that they inevitably colour its dealings with other nations, and so one always finds it regarded as a dubious friend and a tricky foe. That the United States, in its foreign relations, has descended to gross deceits and tergiversations since the earliest days of the Republic was long ago pointed out by Lecky;[19] it is regarded universally to-day as a pious fraud—which is to say, as a Puritan. Nor has England, the next most eminent democratic state, got the name of *perfide Albion*[20] for nothing. Ruled by shady men, a nation itself becomes shady.

In its domestic relations, of course, the same causes have the same effects. The government deals with the citizens from whom it has its mandate in a base and disingenuous manner, and fails completely to maintain equal justice among them. It not only follows the majority in persecuting those who happen to be unpopular; it also institutes persecutions of its own, and frequently against men of the greatest rectitude and largest public usefulness. I marvel that no candidate for the doctorate has ever written a realistic history of the American Department of Justice, ironically so called. It has been engaged in sharp practices since the earliest days, and remains a fecund source of oppression and corruption to-day. It is hard to recall an administration in which it was not the centre of grave scandal. Within our own time it has actually resorted to perjury in its efforts to undo men guilty of flouting it, and at all times it has laboured valiantly to nullify the guarantees of the Bill of Rights. The doings of its corps of spies and *agents provocateurs* are worthy the pen of some confectioner of dime novels; at one time they were employed against the members of the two houses of Congress,[21] and the alarmed legislators threw them off only by threatening to hold up their pay. As Mill[22] long ago pointed out, the tyranny of the majority under democracy is not only shown in oppressive laws, but also in a usurped power to suspend the operation of laws that are just. In this enterprise a democratic government always marches ahead of the majority. Even more than the most absolute oriental despotism, it becomes a government of men, not of laws. Its favourites are, to all intents and purposes, immune to criminal processes, whatever their offences, and its enemies are exposed to espionage and persecution of the most aggravated sort. It takes advantage of every passing craze and delusion of the mob to dispose of those who oppose it, and it maintains a complex and highly effective machine for launching such crazes and delusions when the supply of them lags. Above all, it always shows that characteristically Puritan habit of which Brooks Adams[23] wrote in "The Emancipation of Massachusetts": the habit, to wit, of inflicting as much mental suffering as possible upon its victims. That is to say, it not only has at them by legal means; it also defames them, and so seeks to ruin them doubly. The constant and central aim of every democratic government is to silence criticism of itself. It begins to weaken, *i.e.*, the jobs of its component rogues begin to be insecure, the instant such criticism rises. It is thus *fidei defensor*[24] before it is anything else, and its whole power, legal and extra-legal, is thrown against the sceptic who challenges its infallibility. Constitutional checks have little effect upon its operations, for the only machinery for putting them into effect is under its control. No ruler, indeed, ever wants to be a constitutional ruler, and least of all the ruler whose reign has a term, and who must make hay, in consequence, while the sun shines. Under republics, as under constitutional monarchies, the history of government is a history of successive usurpations. I avoid the banality of pointing to the cases of Lincoln and Wilson.[25] No man would want to be President of the United States in strict accordance with the Constitution. There is no sense of power in merely executing laws; it comes from evading or augmenting them.

I incline to think that this view of government as a group of men struggling for power and profit, in the face and at the expense of the generality of men, has its place somewhere in the dark recesses of the popular mind, and that it accounts, at least in large part, for the toleration with which public corruption is regarded in democratic states. Democratic man, to begin with, is corrupt himself: he will take whatever he can safely get, law or no law. He assumes, naturally and accurately, that the knaves and mountebanks who govern him are of the same kidney—in his own phrase, that they are in public life for what there is in it. It thus does not shock him to find them running true to the ordinances of their nature. If, indeed, any individual among them shows an unusual rectitude, and refuses spectacularly to take what might be his for the grabbing, *Homo boobiens*[26] sets him down as either a liar or an idiot, and refuses to admire him. So with private rogues who tap the communal till. Democratic man is stupid, but he is not so stupid that he does not see the government as a group of men devoted to his exploitation—that is, as a group external to his own group, and with antagonistic interests. He believes that its central aim is to squeeze as much out of him as he can be forced to yield, and so he sees no immorality in attempting a contrary squeeze when the opportunity offers. Beating the government thus becomes a transaction devoid of moral turpitude. If, when it is achieved on an heroic scale by scoundrels of high tone, a storm of public indignation follows, the springs of that indignation are to be found, not in virtue, but in envy. In point of fact, it seldom follows. As I have said, there was little if any public fury over the colossal stealings that went on during the Wilson administration, and there was still less over the smaller but perhaps even more cynical stealings that glorified the short reign of Harding; in the latter case, in fact, most of the odium settled upon the specialists in righteousness who laid the thieves by the heels. The soldiers coming home from the War for Democracy did not demand that the war profiteers be jailed; they simply demanded that they themselves be paid enough to make up the difference between what they got for fighting for their country and what they might have stolen had they escaped the draft. Their chief indignation was lavished, not upon the airship contractors who made off with a billion, but upon their brothers who were paid $10 a day in the shipyards.[27] The feats of the former were beyond their grasp, but those of the latter they could imagine—and envy.

This fellow feeling for thieves is probably what makes capitalism so secure in democratic societies. Under absolutism it is always in danger, and not infrequently, as history teaches, it is exploited and undone, but under democracy it is safe. Democratic man can understand the aims and aspirations of capitalism; they are, greatly magnified, simply his own aims and aspirations.

Thus he tends to be friendly to it, and to view with suspicion those who propose to overthrow it. The new system, whatever its nature, would force him to invent a whole new outfit of dreams, and that is always a difficult and unpleasant business, to workers in the ditch as to philosophers in the learned grove. Capitalism under democracy has a further advantage; its enemies, even when it is attacked, are scattered and weak, and it is usually easily able to array one half of them against the other half, and thus dispose of both. That is precisely what happened in the United States after the late war. The danger that confronted capitalism was then a double one. On the one side there was the tall talk that the returning conscripts, once they got out of uniform, would demand the punishment of the patriots who had looted the public treasury while they were away. On the other side there was an uneasy rumour that a war *Katzenjammer* was heavily upon them, and that they would demand a scientific inquiry into the true causes and aims of the war, and into the manner and purposes of their own uncomfortable exploitation. This double danger was quickly met and turned off, and by the simple device of diverting the bile of the conscripts against those of their own class who had escaped servitude, to wit, the small group of draft-dodgers and conscientious objectors and the larger group of political radicals, who were represented to be slackers in theory if not in fact. Thus one group of victims was set upon the other, and the fact that both had a grievance against their joint exploiters was concealed and forgotten. Mob fears, easily aroused, aided in the achievement of the *coup.* Within a few weeks gallant bands of American Legionaries were hunting Reds down all the back-alleys of the land, and gaudily butchering them, when found, at odds of a hundred to one.[28] I know of nothing more indicative of the strength of capitalism under democracy than* this melodramatic and extremely amusing business. The scheme succeeded admirably, and it

*Correcting "that" in original text.

deserved to succeed, for it was managed with laudable virtuosity, and it was based upon a shrewd understanding of democratic psychology.

I believe that every other emergency that is likely to arise, at least in the United States, will be dealt with in the same adroit and effective manner. The same thing has been done in other democratic states: I point to the so-called general strike in England[29] in 1926, which was wrecked by pitting half of the proletariat against the other half. The capitalistic system now enlists the best brains in all the democratic nations, including France and Germany, and I believe that, instead of losing such support hereafter, it will get more and more of it. As the old aristocracies decline, the plutocracy is bound to inherit their hegemony, and to have the support of the nether mob. An aristocratic society may hold that a soldier or a man of learning is superior to a rich manufacturer or banker, but in a democratic society the latter are inevitably put higher, if *only* because their achievement is more readily comprehended by the inferior man, and he can more easily imagine himself, by some favour of God, duplicating it. Thus the imponderable but powerful force of public opinion directs the aspirations of all the more alert and ambitious young men toward business, and what is so assiduously practised tends to produce experts. E. W. Howe,[30] I incline to think, is quite right when he argues that the average American banker or business man, whatever his demerits otherwise, is at least more competent professionally than the average American statesman, musician, painter, author, labour leader, scholar, theologian or politician. Think of the best American poet of our time, or the best soldier, or the best violoncellist, and then ask yourself if his rank among his fellows in the world is seriously to be compared with that of the late J. Pierpont Morgan among financial manipulators, or that of John D. Rockefeller[31] among traders. The capitalists, in fact, run the country, as they run all democracies: they emerged in Germany, after the republic arose from the ruins of the late war, like Anadyomeme[32] from the sea. They organize and control the minorities that struggle eternally for power, and so get a gradually firmer grip upon the government. One by one they dispose of such demagogues as Bryan and Roosevelt, and put the helm of state into the hands of trusted and reliable men—McKinley,[33] Harding, Coolidge. In England, Germany and France they patronize, in a somewhat wistful way, what remains of the old aristocracies. In the United States, through such agents as the late Gompers,[34] they keep Demos penned in a gilt and glittering cage. Public opinion? Walter Lippmann,[35] searching for it, could not find it. A century before him Fichte said "*es gar nicht existirte.*"[36] Public opinion, in its raw state, gushes out in the immemorial form of the mob's fears. It is piped to central factories, and there it is flavoured and coloured, and put into cans.

IV
Coda

1.
The Future of Democracy

Whether or not democracy is destined to survive in the world until the corruptible puts on incorruption and the immemorial Christian dead leap out of their graves, their faces shining and their yells resounding—this is something, I confess, that I don't know, nor is it necessary, for the purposes of the present inquiry, that I venture upon the hazard of a guess. My business is not prognosis, but diagnosis. I am not engaged in therapeutics, but in pathology. That simple statement of fact, I daresay, will be accepted as a confession, condemning me out of hand as unfit for my task, and even throwing a certain doubt upon my *bona fides*.[1] For it is one of the peculiar intellectual accompaniments of democracy that the concept of the insoluble becomes unfashionable—nay, almost infamous. To lack a remedy is to lack the very license to discuss disease. The causes of this are to be sought, without question, in the nature of democracy itself. It came into the world as a cure-all, and it remains primarily a cure-all to this day. Any boil upon the body politic, however vast and raging, may be relieved by taking a vote; any flux of blood may he stopped by passing a law. The aim of government is to repeal the laws of nature, and re-enact them with moral amendments. War becomes simply a device to end war. The state, a mystical emanation from the mob, takes on a transcendental potency, and acquires the power to make over the father which begat it. Nothing remains inscrutable and beyond remedy, not even the way of a man with a maid. It was not so under the ancient and accursed systems of despotism, now happily purged out of the world. They, too, I grant you, had certain pretensions of an homeric gaudiness, but they at least refrained from attempts to abolish sin, poverty, stupidity, cowardice, and other such immutable realities. Mediæval Christianity, which was a theological and philosophical *apologia* for those systems, actually erected belief in that immutability into a cardinal article of faith. The evils of the world were incurable: one put off the quest for a perfect moral order until one got to heaven, *post mortem.* There arose, in consequence, a scheme of checks and balances that was consummate and completely satisfactory, for it could not be put to a test, and the logical holes in it were chinked with miracles. But no more. To-day the Holy Saints are deposed. Now each and every human problem swings into the range of practical politics. The worst and oldest of them may be solved facilely by travelling bands of lady Ph.D.'s, each bearing the mandate of a Legislature of kept men, all unfaithful to their protectors.

Democracy becomes a substitute for the old religion, and the antithesis of it: the Ku Kluxers, though their reasoning may be faulty, are not far off the facts in their conclusion that Holy Church[2] is its enemy. It shows all the magical potency of the great systems of faith. It has the power to enchant and disarm; it is not vulnerable to logical attack. I point for proof to the appalling gyrations and contortions of its chief exponents. Read, for example, the late James Bryce's "Modern Democracies."[3] Observe how he amasses incontrovertible evidence that democracy doesn't work—and then concludes with a stout declaration that it does. Or, if his two fat volumes are too much for you, turn to some school reader and give a judicious perusal to Lincoln's Gettysburg Address,[4] with its argument that the North fought the Civil War to save self-government to the world!—a thesis echoed in falsetto, and by feebler men, fifty years later. It is impossible, by any device known to philosophers, to meet doctrines of that sort; they obviously lie outside the range of logical ideas. There is, in the human mind, a natural taste for such hocus-pocus. It greatly simplifies the process of ratiocination, which is unbearably painful to the great majority of men. What dulls and baffles the teeth may be got down conveniently by an heroic gulp. No doubt there is an explanation here of the long-continued popularity of the dogma of the Trinity,[5] which remains unstated in plain terms after two thousand years. And no doubt the dogma of Transubstantiation[6] came under fire in the Reformation[7] because it had grown too simple and comprehensible—because even the Scholastic philosophy[8] had been unable to convert its plain propositions into something that could be believed without being understood. Democracy is shot through with this delight in the incredible, this banal mysticism. One cannot discuss it without colliding with preposterous postulates, all of them cherished like authentic hairs from the whiskers of Moses himself. I have alluded to its touching acceptance of the faith that progress is illimitable and ordained of God—that every human problem, in the very nature of things, may be solved. There are corollaries that are even more naïve. One, for example, is to the general effect that optimism is a virtue in itself—that there is a mysterious merit in being hopeful and of glad heart, even in the presence of adverse and immovable fads. This curious notion turns the glittering wheels of Rotary, and is the motive power of the political New Thoughters[9] called Liberals. Certainly the attitude of the average American Liberal toward the so-called League of Nations offered superb clinical material to the student of democratic psychopathology. He began by arguing that the League would save the world. Confronted by proofs of its fraudulence, he switched to the doctrine that believing in it would save the world. So, later on, with the Washington Disarmament Conference.[10] The man who hopes absurdly, it appears, is in some fantastic and gaseous manner a better citizen than the man who detects and exposes the truth. Bear this sweet democratic axiom clearly in mind. It is, fundamentally, what is the matter with the United States.

As I say, my present mandate does not oblige me to conjure up a system that will surpass and shame democracy as democracy surpasses and shames the polity of the Andaman Islanders[11] or the Great Khan[12]—a system full-blown and perfect, like Prohibition, and ready to be put into effect by the simple adoption of an amendment to the Constitution. Such a system, for all I know, may lie outside the farthest soarings of the human mind, though that mind can weigh the stars and know God. Until the end of the chapter the ants and bees may flutter their sardonic antennæ at us in that department, as they do in others: the last joke upon man may be that he never learned how to govern himself in a rational and competent manner, as the last joke upon woman may be that she never had a baby without wishing that the Day of Judgment were a week past. I am not even undertaking to prove here that democracy is too full of evils to be further borne. On the contrary, I am convinced that it has some valuable merits, not often described, and I shall refer to a few of them presently. All I argue is that its manifest defects, if they are ever to he got rid of at all, must be got rid of by examining them realistically—that they will never cease to afflict all the more puissant and exemplary nations so long as discussing them is impeded by concepts borrowed from theology. As for me, I have never encountered any actual evidence, convincing to an ordinary jury, that *vox populi* is actually *vox Dei.*[13] The proofs, indeed, run the other way. The life of the inferior man is one long protest against the obstacles that God interposes to the attainment of his dreams, and democracy, if it is anything at all, is simply one way of getting 'round those obstacles. Thus it represents, not a jingling echo of what seems to be the divine will, but a raucous defiance of it. To that extent, perhaps, it is truly civilized, for civilization, as I have argued elsewhere, is best described as an effort to remedy the blunders and check the cruel humours of the Cosmic Kaiser. But what is defiant is surely not official, and what is not official is open to examination.

For all I know, democracy may be a self-limiting disease, as civilization itself seems to be. There are obvious parodoxes in its philosophy, and some of them have a suicidal smack. It offers John Doe a means to rise above his place beside Richard Roe, and then, by making Roe his equal, it takes away the chief usufructs of the rising. I here attempt no pretty logical gymnastics: the history of democratic states is a history of disingenuous efforts to get rid of the second half of that dilemma. There is not only the natural yearning of Doe to use and enjoy the superiority that he has won; there is also the natural tendency of Roe, as an inferior man, to acknowledge it. Democracy, in fact, is always inventing class distinctions, despite its theoretical abhorrence of them. The baron has departed, but in his place stand the grand goblin, the supreme worthy archon, the sovereign grand commander.[14] Democratic man, as I have remarked, is quite unable to think of himself as a free individual; he must belong to a group, or shake with fear and loneliness—and the group, of course, must have its leaders. It would be hard to find a country in which such brummagem serene highnesses are revered with more passionate devotion than they get in the United States. The distinction that goes with mere office runs far ahead of the distinction that goes with actual achievement. A Harding is regarded as genuinely superior to a Halsted,[15] no doubt because his doings are better understood. But there is a form of human striving that is understood by democratic man even better than Harding's, and that is the striving for money. Thus the plutocracy, in a democratic state, tends to take the place of the missing aristocracy, and even to be mistaken for it. It is, of course, something quite different. It lacks all the essential characters of a true aristorcracy: a clean tradition, culture, public spirit, honesty, honour, courage—above all, courage. It stands under no bond of obligation to the state; it has no public duty; it is transient and lacks a goal. Its most puissant dignitaries of to-day came out of the mob only yesterday—and from the mob they bring all its peculiar ignobilities. As practically encountered, the plutocracy stands quite as far from the *honnête homme*[16] as it stands from the Holy Saints. Its main character is its incurable timorousness; it is for ever grasping at the straws held out by demagogues. Half a dozen gabby Jewish youths, meeting in a back room to plan a revolution—in other words, half a dozen kittens preparing to upset the Matterhorn[17]—are enough to scare it half to death. Its dreams are of banshees, hobgoblins, bugaboos. The honest, untroubled snores of a Percy or a Hohenstaufen[18] are quite beyond it.

The plutocracy, as I say, is comprehensible to the mob because its aspirations are essentially those of inferior men: it is not by accident that Christianity, a mob religion, paves heaven with gold and precious stones, *i. e.*, with money. There are, of course, reactions against this ignoble ideal among men of more civilized tastes, even in democratic states, and sometimes they arouse the mob to a transient distrust of certain of the plutocratic pretensions. But that distrust seldom arises above mere envy, and the polemic which engenders it is seldom sound in logic or impeccable in motive. What it lacks is aristocratic disinterestedness, born of aristocratic security. There is no body of opinion behind it that is, in the strictest sense, a free opinion. Its chief exponents, by some divine irony, are pedagogues of one sort or another—which is to say, men chiefly marked by their haunting fear of losing their jobs. Living under such terrors, with the plutocracy policing them harshly on one side and the mob congenitally suspicious of them on the other, it is no wonder that their revolt usually peters out in metaphysics, and that they tend to abandon it as their families grow up, and the costs of heresy become prohibitive. The pedagogue, in the long run, shows the virtues of the Congressman, the newspaper editorial writer or the butler, not those of the aristocrat. When, by any chance, he persists in contumacy beyond thirty, it is only too commonly a sign, not that he is heroic, but simply that he is pathological. So with most of his brethren of the Utopian Fife and Drum Corps, whether they issue out of his own seminary or out of the wilderness. They are fanatics; not statesmen. Thus politics, under democracy, resolves itself into impossible alternatives. Whatever the label on the parties, or the war cries issuing from the demagogues who lead them, the practical choice is between the plutocracy on the one side and a rabble of preposterous impossibilists on the other. One must either follow the New York *Times*, or one must he prepared to swallow Bryan and the Bolsheviki. It is a pity that this is so. For what democracy needs most of all is a party that will separate the good that is in it theoretically from the evils that beset it practically, and then try to erect that good into a workable system. What it needs beyond everything is a party of liberty. It produces, true enough, occasional libertarians, just as despotism produces occasional regicides, but it treats them in the same drum-head way. It will never have a party of them until it invents and installs a genuine aristocracy, to breed them and secure them.

2.
Last Words

I have alluded somewhat vaguely to the merits of democracy. One of them is quite obvious: it is, perhaps, the most charming form of government ever devised by man. The reason is not far to seek. It is based upon propositions that are palpably not true—and what is not true, as everyone knows, is always immensely more fascinating and satisfying to the vast majority of men than what is true. Truth has a harshness that alarms them, and an air of finality that collides with their incurable romanticism. They turn, in all the great emergencies of life, to the ancient promises, transparently false but immensely comforting, and of all those ancient promises there is none more comforting than the one to the effect that the lowly shall inherit the earth. It is at the bottom of the dominant religious system of the modern world, and it is at the bottom of the dominant political system. The latter, which is democracy, gives it an even higher credit and authority than the former, which is Christianity. More, democracy gives it a certain appearance of objective and demonstrable truth. The mob man, functioning as citizen, gets a feeling that he is really important to the world—that he is genuinely running things. Out of his maudlin herding after rogues and mountebanks there comes to him a sense of vast and mysterious power—which is what makes archbishops, police sergeants, the grand goblins of the Ku Klux and other such magnificoes happy. And out of it there comes, too, a conviction that he is somehow wise, that his views are taken seriously by his betters—which is what makes United States Senators, fortunetellers and Young Intellectuals[1] happy. Finally, there comes out of it a glowing consciousness of a high duty triumphantly done—which is what makes hangmen and husbands happy.

All these forms of happiness, of course, are illusory. They don't last. The democrat, leaping into the air to flap his wings and praise God, is for ever coming down with a thump. The seeds of his disaster, as I have shown, lie in his own stupidity: he can never get rid of the naïve delusion—so beautifully Christian!—that happiness is something to be got by taking it away from the other fellow. But there are seeds, too, in the very nature of things: a promise, after all, is only a promise, even when it is supported by divine revelation, and the chances against its fulfilment may be put into a depressing mathematical formula. Here the irony that lies under all human aspiration shows itself: the quest for happiness, as always, brings only unhappiness in the end. But saying that is merely saying that the true charm of democracy is not for the democrat but for the spectator. That spectator, it seems to me, is favoured with a show of the first cut and calibre. Try to imagine anything more heroically absurd! What grotesque false pretences! What a parade of obvious imbecilities! What a welter of fraud! But is fraud unamusing? Then I retire forthwith as a psychologist. The fraud of democracy, I contend, is more amusing than any other—more amusing even, and by miles, than the fraud of religion. Go into your praying-chamber and give sober thought to any of the more characteristic democratic inventions: say, Law Enforcement. Or to any of the typical democratic prophets: say, the late Archangel Bryan. If you don't come out paled and palsied by mirth then you will not laugh on the Last Day itself, when Presbyterians step out of the grave like chicks from the egg, and wings blossom from their scapulæ,[2] and they leap into interstellar space with roars of joy.

I have spoken hitherto of the possibility that democracy may be a self-limiting disease, like measles. It is, perhaps, something more: it is self-devouring. One cannot observe it objectively without being impressed by its curious distrust of itself—its apparently ineradicable tendency to abandon its whole philosophy at the first sign of strain. I need not point to what happens invariably in democratic states when the national safety is menaced. All the great tribunes of democracy, on such occasions, convert themselves, by a process as simple as taking a deep breath, into despots of an almost fabulous ferocity. Lincoln, Roosevelt and Wilson come instantly to mind: Jackson[3] and Cleveland[4] are in the background, waiting to be recalled. Nor is this process confined to times of alarm and terror: it is going on day in and day out. Democracy always seems bent upon killing the thing it theoretically loves. I have rehearsed some of its operations against liberty, the very cornerstone of its political metaphysic. It not only wars upon the thing itself; it even wars upon mere academic advocacy of it. I offer the spectacle of Americans jailed for reading the Bill of Rights[5] as perhaps the most gaudily humorous ever witnessed in the modern world. Try to imagine monarchy jailing subjects for maintaining the divine right of Kings! Or Christianity damning a believer for arguing that Jesus Christ was the Son of God! This last, perhaps, has been done: anything is possible in that direction. But under democracy the remotest and most fantastic possibility is a commonplace of every day. All the axioms resolve themselves into thundering paradoxes, many amounting to downright contradictions in terms. The mob is competent to rule the rest of us—but it must be rigorously policed itself. There is a government, not of men, but of laws—but men are set upon benches to decide finally what the law is and may be. The highest function of the citizen is to serve the state—but the first assumption that meets him, when he essays to discharge it, is an assumption of his disingenuousness and dishonour. Is that assumption commonly sound? Then the farce only grows the more glorious.

I confess, for my part, that it greatly delights me. I enjoy democracy immensely. It is incomparably idiotic, and hence incomparably amusing. Does it exalt dunderheads, cowards, trimmers, frauds, cads? Then the pain of seeing them go up is balanced and obliterated by the joy of seeing them come down. Is it inordinately wasteful, extravagant, dishonest? Then so is every other form of government: all alike are enemies to laborious and virtuous men. Is rascality at the very heart of it? Well, we have borne that rascality since 1776, and continue to survive. In the long run, it may turn out that rascality is necessary to human government, and even to civilization itself—that civilization, at bottom, is nothing but a colossal swindle.[6] I do not know: I report only that when the suckers are running well the spectacle is infinitely exhilarating. But I am, it may be, a somewhat malicious man: my sympathies, when it comes to suckers, tend to be coy. What I can't make out is how any man can believe in democracy who feels for and with them, and is pained when they are debauched and made a show of. How can any man be a democrat who is sincerely a democrat?

THE END

Annotations

I. DEMOCRATIC MAN

1. *His Appearance in the World*

1. ***Rousseau's noble savage*** Jean-Jacques Rousseau (1712–1778). French philosopher. Although aware a return to the primitive state was impractical, Rousseau used the myth of the noble savage to give substance to his diatribes against civilization.

2. ***Modernism*** A tendency in theology to accommodate traditional religious teaching with contemporary thought, and especially to devalue the supernatural.

3. ***Liberals*** Mencken thought liberals clung to figments of imagination, with "a kind of hope that far surpasses a Seventh Day Adventist's." In 1924 he wrote, liberals see "the world from first to last through an amber and palpitating haze. . . . They are often acutely intelligent . . . and for certain kinds of sham, they have sharp eyes, but to other kinds they are completely blind. Always they cling to some shred of illusion, as if the whole truth were too harsh to be borne, and often it is a shred indeed."

4. ***acroamatic*** Pertaining to deep learning.

5. ***the Paris proletariat . . . de jure*** A complex interplay of government impotence, social injustice and economic hardship actuated the French Revolution. In 1792 a Paris insurrection overthrew the monarchy. The next year King Louis XVI was executed. The Reign of Terror, a period of brutal repression, aimed to chase the Revolution's enemies from France. Estimates put its death toll between 18,500 to 40,000 lives. By 1796 the Reign was over, but the new government of the Directory lasted only four years. In 1799 a coup d'etat brought forth Napoleon Bonaparte, soon to be France's first emperor; ***de jure*** by law (Latin).

6. ***By 1828 in America and 1848 in Europe . . .*** Andrew Jackson (1767–1845) unseated John Quincy Adams (1767–1848) in the 1828 presidential election. Jackson was a self-made man of modest wealth from the western frontier and an icon of the ascendancy of the "common man" in American politics. Previous presidents had been from the East, born to patrician and wealthy families. Historians view this election as marking the coming-of-age of a huge majority of Americans. However, Mencken saw Jackson's victory in much the same way as Henry Adams (1838–1918), a historian and John Quincy's grandson. Henry Adams observed, "[A]fter General [George] Washington died, the democratic system of averages began its work, and the old inequality sank to the common level. By 1828, a level of degradation had been reached, and it was the level of Jackson." It was "a fall in intelligence and intellectual energy of the democratic community" that had once been elevated by George Washington and John Quincy, "who perfectly appreciated the catastrophe, and felt it." For Europe 1848 was a watershed, marking a revolutionary year affecting France, Germany, Italy, and Poland as the common people fought for social and economic change.

7. ***In 1867 a philosopher out of the gutter . . . conclusion*** Karl Marx (1818–1883), the father of modern Communism, published the first volume of *Das Kapital* in 1867. It is an extensive examination of political economy and society, with a critical analysis of capitalism. Marx viewed capitalism as the exploitation and alienation of labor. In *Chrestomathy,* Mencken revised this line to "a philosopher out of the ghetto." See *A Mencken Chrestomathy* (New York: Vintage Books, 1982), p. 156

8. ***The late war*** World War I.

2. *Varieties of Homo Sapiens*

1. ***intelligence tests*** At the turn of the century there was a rise in the social significance of hereditary characteristics. Eugenics was one of the most enduring aspects of social Darwinism. Popular credulity about the scope and variety of hereditary traits was almost boundless. In *Men Versus the Man* Mencken tackled notions about the relationship of genetics, intelligence, and race. When eugenics became a worldwide movement in the 1920s, with planning committees heavily involved in race betterment, he found much to criticize. In this passage, Mencken refers to a piece he wrote for the *Chicago Tribune* ("Intelligence Tests," July 5, 1925). He said intelligence tests were full of "gross defects. Only too often they mistake information for intelligence."

2. ***MM. Simon and Binet*** Mencken used certain phrases repeatedly: "the hon. gentleman," "the rev. clergy," and, in this instance, "MM" for "messieurs." Alfred Binet (1857–1911) and Théodore Simon (1873–1961), French psychologists. Together they developed an evaluation of child mental development by a series of psychological tests. The Simon-Binet Scale became the standard intelligence test in the U.S. and was widely used in the 1920s. "IQ," an abbreviation of Binet and Simon's term "intelligence quotient," entered the vocabulary.

3. ***Holy Alliance*** A coalition of Russia, Austria, and Prussia created in 1815 at the behest of Czar Alexander I, with the goal of instilling the Christian values of justice, love, and peace. Except for Great Britain, other European countries joined, making it the first modern international peacekeeping organization. It became defunct with Alexander's death in 1825.

4. ***Little Bethel*** Bethel was a historic city and ceremonial center near Jerusalem. In the U.S. some churches are named "Little Bethel" in its honor.

5. ***Genesis I, 27*** "So God created man in his own image, in the image of God created he him; male and female created he them."

6. ***Fundamentalists*** Christians who believe sacred scripture is the literal word of God. In the 1920s, Fundamentalism's social roots were most apparent in the South.

7. ***Charles Richet*** French physiologist (1850–1935). He won the Nobel Prize for medicine in 1913 for his work on serum therapy, which threw new light on such diseases as hay fever and asthma.

8. ***Homo stultus*** "Foolish man" (Latin).

3. *The New Psychology*

1. ***Golf . . . Americanism*** Americans in the 1920s had more time and money to play sports, especially golf. It caught on so quickly that by 1927 there were 5,000 golf courses and two million players, and the number grew every year. To Mencken, golf and idiocy were slightly different forms of the same thing. Mencken harbored a similar disdain for other phenomena of the decade. He viewed the followers of Fundamentalism as "frauds," osteopaths as "quacks," and the aims of the National Association of Rotary Clubs, formed in 1910 by business leaders to foster goodwill, as consisting of "bilge." By 1922 Rotary had expanded its branches into six continents, and changed its name to Rotary International.

The term "Americanism" was commonly used to connote an uncritical, hyperpatriotism at a time of great xenophobia. (The 1919 Pulitzer Prize for public service was awarded to the *Milwaukee Journal* for "its strong and courageous campaign for Americanism in a constituency where foreign elements made such a policy hazardous from a business point of view.")

For Mencken, golf, Rotary, Fundamentalism, and osteopathy were typical American amusements and values. "Any man who believes in osteopathy, chiropractic, thought transference, table tapping, international peace, the divinity of Christ, the Coolidge legend or any such chimera is very offensive to me," he once wrote. He despised "credulous men" who "succumbed" to "every fresh fraud that comes along." When it came to osteopathy especially, Mencken had little patience; for him, the hard sciences were everything.

2. ***old-time introspective psychology*** Nineteenth-century psychology relied on introspection. It was challenged by German psychologist Wilhelm Wundt (1832–1920), founder of cognitive psychology. Under Wundt's method, reactions to stimuli, such as colors and sounds, were observed and measured. In *Principles of Physiological Psychology*, Wundt wrote that trained professionals must make observations under precise conditions to answer specific questions. This method is still followed today.

3. ***The behaviourists*** An approach to psychology based on the proposition that behavior can be studied and explained scientifically as a physiological response to stimuli, without recourse to mental states.

4. ***Dr. John B. Watson*** (1878–1958) Psychologist. Watson was a professor of experimental and comparative psychology at Johns Hopkins University, located in Mencken's hometown of Baltimore. He was the founder of the behaviorist school of psychology.

5. ***Dr. Eleanor R. Wembridge*** (1882–1944) American psychologist.

4. *Politics Under Democracy*

1. ***snooper*** One who investigates or monitors in an official capacity, often nosily. The *Oxford English Dictionary* cites as an example a sentence from a 1928 *Chicago Tribune* article: "Prohibition Commissioner Doran has warned dry snoopers to stop gunplay against innocent citizens."

2. ***The whole history . . . Bolshevism*** Mencken wrote that

"Civilization, in fact, grows more and more maudlin and hysterical, and especially under democracy it tends to degenerate into a mere combat of crazes. The whole aim of practical politics is to keep the populace alarmed (and hence clamorous to be led to safety) by menacing it with an endless series of hobgoblins, all of them imaginary." (From *In Defense of Women*, excerpted in *Chrestomathy*, page 29.) Here Mencken cites a few of these "hobgoblins": ***red-coats*** British soldiers who fought the Patriots during the American Revolution; ***Hessians*** German mercenaries retained by the British during the Revolution; ***monocrats*** Thomas Jefferson decried the efforts of Alexander Hamilton and other Federalists to develop a powerful central government as a betrayal of the Revolution, and claimed their aim was to establish a ruling class of "monocrats"; ***the Bank*** The First Bank of the United States, founded by Alexander Hamiton; ***the Catholics*** throughout American history there is a strain of prejudice against Catholics, and the 1920s were no exception. Many saw Catholics as foreign, and felt a vote for a Catholic presidential candidate, like New York governor Al Smith in the 1928 election, was a vote for the Pope; ***Simon Legree*** a character from Harriet Beecher Stowe's novel, *Uncle Tom's Cabin*, synonymous with cruelty toward blacks; ***the Slave Power*** a term used from 1840 to 1865 in the North for slaveholders' political might; ***Jeff Davis*** Jefferson Davis (1808–1889). The Confederacy's president (1861–1865); ***Mormonism*** like Catholics, Mormons were often regarded with distrust; ***Wall Street*** America's financial center; ***the rum demon*** Mencken pokes fun at the temperance movement, which considered all alcohol Satanic; ***John Bull*** Great Britain personified; ***General Weyler*** Valeriano Weyler (1830–1930) of the Spanish Army, who fought against Cuban rebels and placed them in "reconcentration" camps, outraging Americans, who sided with the rebels in the Spanish-American War of 1898; ***Pancho Villa*** Doroteo Arayo Arámbula (1878–1923). The Mexican Revolution's best known general, who personally led a 1916 raid on Columbus, New Mexico; ***German spies*** although there were German spies in America during World War I, Mencken takes issue with hysteria against all Germans; ***hyphenates*** Immigrants and their children, such as Italian-Americans, Irish-Americans, etc. It described people suspected of divided loyalties. Theodore Roosevelt gave a speech against "Hyphenated Americanism" in 1915; ***the Kaiser*** Wilhelm II (1859–1941). Last Emperor of Germany, whose army fought against the Allies in World War I; ***Bolshevism*** an early term for Marxist-Leninism.

3. ***Bryan, Roosevelt and Wilson*** William Jennings Bryan (1860–1925) was a fundamentalist political leader, secretary of state under Woodrow Wilson (1913–1915), and three-time Democratic presidential nominee. Taking issue with the strident wording of Wilson's second note to Germany following the sinking of the *Lusitania*, Bryan resigned from his post as secretary of state in 1915. However, he supported Wilson's bid for a second term and even volunteered for military service when the U.S. entered World War I. (He was rejected.) He campaigned for Prohibition and women's right to vote.

Theodore Roosevelt (1858–1919). President (R, 1901-1909). He was widely admired in his day for his boundless gusto and jingoistic nationalism.

Woodrow Wilson (1856–1924). President (D, 1913-1921). Throughout his first term, Wilson avoided involvement in the "Great War," and campaigned for his second term on the slogan "He Kept Us Out of War." As the conflict continued, news of German atrocities and the sinkings of the British steamer *Lusitania* and the U.S.S. *Housatonic* prompted Wilson to call for a declaration of a "war to end all wars." Mencken was no great fan of Wilson, "who looked like a Sunday school teacher" but was actually "a witch burner." Mencken resented the hysterical patriotism that was whipped up by Wilson's powerful propaganda machine, the Committee on Public Information. It was headed by George Creel (1876–1953), who later admitted to fabricating stories. Wilson's administration censored, intimidated, and imprisoned critics of the war and turned a blind eye to the mistreatment of German-Americans and African-American dissidents. It also ignored the steady increase of lynching of blacks in the South.

4. ***so-called constructive program*** Bryan's cause of "free silver" in his 1896 presidential campaign won him support among many Americans, especially farmers. Bryan felt the value of the dollar should be pegged to silver instead of gold, to make it easier for farmers to pay off their debts. Opposition to his plan came from wealthy men as well as employers, who thought free silver would ruin the economy. Factory owners shut down some of their plants and threatened to shut others if Bryan was elected. Many voters, now facing an economic downturn, decided they could not risk their livelihood by voting for "The Great Commoner."

5. ***cross-of-gold speech*** A reference to Bryan's famous nomination speech at the 1896 Democratic National Convention in Chicago. A skillful orator, he electrified the audience. Bryan viewed the gold

standard as a struggle between the cities and the countryside, good versus evil. Prosperous city men favored gold at the cost of poor rural workers. He ended his address with "You shall not press down upon the brow of labor this crown of thorns, you shall not crucify mankind upon a cross of gold," and dramatically held out his arms as one crucified.

6. ***evolutionary hypothesis*** The theory of evolution by natural selection was first argued by the naturalist Charles Robert Darwin (1809–1882). It is the process by which a species of plants or animals gradually develops over a period of many generations from a simple to a complex form of organism. Detailed in *On The Origin of Species by Means of Natural Selection*, it aroused a storm of controversy. In *The Descent of Man*, Darwin advanced the theory that humans evolved from anthropoids.

Tennessee in 1925 was the first state to enact legislation against teaching the theory of evolution in public schools. After reading that the American Civil Liberties Union sought a teacher to fight the law, a local businessman convinced Dayton, Tennessee's school board to recruit a teacher to lecture on Darwin's theory, both to impugn the law and give the town's economy an anticipated boost through publicity. John Scopes was arrested for teaching Darwin's theory to his high school biology class.

The battle gained national prominence when the ACLU hired famed lawyer Clarence Darrow (1857–1938) to defend Scopes and challenge the constitutionality of a law that violated free speech and the separation of church and state. The Christian Fundamentalist Organization asked William Jennings Bryan to help with the prosecution. The ensuing trial held the nation's attention and raised important issues of religious freedom, the separation of church and state, and free speech. It was presided over by John Raulston, a local judge. During the trial the small town became a feverish home for the press. Mencken himself covered the proceedings for the Baltimore *Evening Sun.* Scopes was found guilty and fined $100. The conviction was overturned by the Tennessee Supreme Court on a technicality. The trial was later dramatized in the play *Inherit the Wind*. When it was made into a film, Gene Kelly played a journalist modeled after Mencken.

7. ***But he allowed his foes*** On the trial's last day, Darrow called in Bryan as a witness, and interrogated him with questions that tested the Bible's historical authenticity. It was a humiliating ordeal for Bryan, who died a few days later. "[H]inds" (*i.e.*, "rustics") is less a crit-

icism of the locals than Mencken's view of Raulston and Bryan's colleagues in the prosecution team. Mencken warned his readers not to look upon the Scopes trial as merely a "trivial farce," saying it had far-reaching implications.

8. ***The most popular song, in the United States, in 1915*** "I Didn't Raise My Boy To Be A Soldier," written by Alfred Bryan before the U.S. entry into World War I, was a number one hit. It sparked controversy, and incited composers to write other songs in response, opposing Bryan's anti-war sentiments.

9. ***No ship went down*** The *Lusitania* was a British-owned liner that was torpedoed without warning and sunk by a German submarine off the coast of Ireland in May 1915. A total of 1,153 passengers died, among them 128 Americans. Afterward anti-German feeling ran high. In America, the teaching of German was banned from schools; one Iowa politician charged "ninety-nine percent of all men and women who taught German were traitors." German books were burned, German newspapers were censored, and German clubs disappeared. Local epidemics were blamed on the local water supply's contamination by German spies. In Congress a resolution was introduced to eliminate German names from cities. Many Germans changed their names, as from "Schmidt" to "Smith."

5. *The Rôle of the Hormones*

1. ***Freud*** Sigmund Freud (1856–1939). Austrian neurologist and founder of the psychoanalytic school of psychology. *Three Essays on the Theory of Sexuality* advanced his theory on sexuality, especially in childhood.

2. **sage-femme** "Wise woman." (French)

3. ***wormed through the mails*** "Sneaked" through the mails. In Mencken's time some publications were deprived of their mailing privileges for alleged decency violations. In every case the post office was both the prosecutor and judge. Quite often post office attorneys sought to show the magazines were not only obscene but lewd.

4. ***Torquemada*** Tomás de Torquemada (1420–1498). Spanish Dominican and Inquisitor General. His role in the Spanish Inquisition made his name a byword for cruelty and fanaticism in the service of Catholicism.

5. ***The American Legion*** World War I veterans founded the American Legionnaires in 1919, also known as the American Legion.

Congress awarded it a charter. Rep Hamilton Fish, Jr. (1888–1991; R-N.Y, 1919–1944) declared the Legion was pledged to "foster and perpetuate one hundred percent Americanism." By the spring of 1919 the press was filled with lurid stories about Russian Bolshevists and their threat to the nation. "The Red Scare" reached such proportions that the American Legion joined forces with the Justice Department to curb radicalism, both real and imagined. Some 6,000 citizens were illegally detained. With the help of the Legion, as well as state governments, businesses, and private detective agencies, the Department set forth a series of anti-labor and anti-radical attacks known as the "Palmer raids", after Alexander Mitchell Palmer (1872–1936), attorney general (1919–1921). Much of the aggression was directed at immigrants. Over the next few months, 150,000 radical leaders, organizations and publications were scrutinized. There were massive round-ups. Some were beaten up, jailed and deported. Mencken wrote some of his strongest newspaper articles against this repression when he launched his "Monday Articles" column in the Baltimore *Evening* Sun in 1920. He refers to this period again on pp. 141-142.

6. ***In a previous work . . . peasants*** Mencken alludes to *Men Versus the Man: A Correspondence Between Roves La Monte, Socialist, and H. L. Mencken, Individualist* (New York: Holt, 1910).

7. ***That theory . . . attorney-general*** Arthur Thomas Stewart (1892–1972). District attorney for the 18th Circuit in Tennessee and chief prosecutor in the Scopes trial. He later served as a U.S. senator (D-Tenn., 1939–1949).

8. ***the alpha and omega . . . the farm*** Mencken most likely refers to the Tariff Act of 1922, which he lambasted in his editorial in the March 1924 *American Mercury* (pp. 293-296). "Has anyone ever heard of a farmer making any sacrifice of his own interests, however slight, to the common good?" he wrote. "When the going is good he robs the rest of us up the extreme limit of our endurance; when the going is bad he comes bawling for help out of the public till." Mencken's disdain for the farmer is evident in all of his writing.

9. ***the trappings of Service*** Mencken is sarcastic. He is probably referring to the Rotary's motto: "Service above Self."

6. *Envy As a Philosophy*

1. ***"l'envie," as Heine said to Philarète Chasles, "est une infériorité qui s'avoue."*** "Envy is an inferiority to which one must

submit." (French); Heinrich Heine (1797–1856). German poet; Philarete Chasles (1798–1873). French critic.

2. ***lilies-of-the-valley, Jockey Club*** Two English perfumes.

3. ***friendly bumper*** a cup or glass filled to the brim.

4. ***yellow-backs as "Night Life in Chicago"*** A "yellowback" was a cheap, sensational book with a yellow cover. Mencken may be referring to *Life in Chicago, or, Day and Night in the World's Wickedest City, Containing Many Graphic Sketches*, written "by an ex-detective" and published in 1876. It was advertised as an exposé of the highest crust of Chicago society and of "female innocence, taken from life, etc. etc." Mencken defined the popular seller as "a cheap book . . . of frankly pornographic character." When, as he put it, "yokels read at all, it is commonly such garbage that they prefer."

5. ***Pfeffers*** Mencken probably is referring to (and misspelling the name of) William Alfred Peffer (1831–1912), a Populist senator from Kansas serving from 1881 to 1897.

6. ***Mann Act*** Named after its sponsor, Rep. James Robert Mann (1856–1922; R-Ill, 1897–1922), the White Slave Traffic Act of 1910 banned the transportation of women across state lines "for the purpose of prostitution or debauchery, or for any other immoral purpose."

7. ***panem et circenses*** "Bread and circuses" (Latin). The phrase is thought coined by Juvenal, the satiric poet of the first century, to describe the Roman emperors' practice of providing unlimited free wheat and costly circus games to pacify the poor.

8. ***third theological virtue*** The third virtue's definition varies with English translations of the Bible. In the Geneva Bible, 1 Corinthians 13:13 explains: "And now abideth faith, hope and love, even those three: but the chiefest of them is love." In the King James version the third virtue is "charity."

9. ***decidua serotina*** A part of the uterus' membrane that develops into the placenta's maternal section.

10. ***yellow journalism*** Rival publishers William Randolph Hearst (1863–1951) and Joseph Pulitzer (1847–1911) competed over whose newspaper could better dramatize Spanish injustices in Cuba. Hearst and Pulitzer's type of reporting was known as "yellow journalism." From it came America's war with Spain in 1898, and a new surge in growth for the newspaper business.

11. ***Knickerbocker*** A descendant of the original Dutch settlers of Manhattan, then known as New Amsterdam.

7. *Liberty and Democratic Man*

1. ***panem et circenses*** "Bread and circuses" (Latin). See Note 7 to Part I, Chapter 6.

2. ***Frederick the Great*** Frederick II (1712–1786). King of Prussia (1740–1786). He embraced the principles of the Enlightenment, with its emphasis on rationality. Frederick allowed religious toleration, freedom of speech and the press, and encouraged arts and education. In doing so, he transformed Prussia into an economically strong and politically reformed state.

3. ***than Thomas Paine made*** English-born Thomas Paine (1737–1809) immigrated to the Colonies in 1774. He took part in the American Revolution as the author of *Common Sense*, a pamphlet that advocated independence from Great Britain. He outlined his political philosophy in the controversial *Rights of Man.* The influential tome was published in 1791, the same year Paine moved to France. His enthusiastic support of the French Revolution earned him honorary citizenship and election to the National Convention. Eventually he fell into disfavor, and was arrested and imprisoned. He narrowly escaped execution when the chalk mark on his cell's door—designating him as next in line for the guillotine—was overlooked by the guards. Paine was released, due in large part to the work of the new American minister to France, James Monroe.

4. ***natural manure*** "The tree of liberty must be refreshed from time to time with the blood of patriots and tyrants. It is its natural manure." Thomas Jefferson, Letter to W. S. Smith, November 13, 1787.

5. ***Homo boobiens*** A play on Mencken's term "booboisie": the ignorant masses.

6. ***Ludwig van Beethoven*** See Note 19 to Part I, Chapter 8.

7. ***honour*** Mencken felt very strongly about the term. He once commented: "[In] the United States . . . the word honor, save when it is applied to the structural integrity of women, has only a comic significance. When one hears of the honor of politicians, of bankers, of lawyers, of the United States itself, everyone naturally laughs." (Baltimore *Evening Sun*, August 30, 1926, excerpted in *Chrestomathy*, page 282.)

8. ***Sir Francis Galton*** (1822–1911). Half-cousin of Charles Darwin, best known for his work in anthropology and for his study of heredity. Considered the founder of eugenics, a term he coined,

Galton was the first to apply statistical methods to the study of the inheritance of intelligence. Mencken quotes from *Inquiries Into Human Faculty and Its Development*, 2nd Ed. (New York: E.P. Dutton & Co., 1908), p. 47.

9. ***universal . . . 1867*** In Colonial times voting was restricted to property owners and taxpayers. The Reconstruction Act of 1867 mandated that each state constitution must allow all male citizens to vote, regardless of race. Three years later the 15th Amendment was passed, guaranteeing the right of African-American men to vote. However, through poll taxes and other methods, including outright violence, blacks were essentially barred from voting in the South for another century. The 19th Amendment (1920) opened voting to women.

8. *The Effects Upon Progress*

1. ***American Federation of Labour*** Many Americans were convinced that Bolsheviks were behind the American Federation of Labor (Mencken uses the British spelling of "labor.") To some this Red-baiting smear was plausible as many union members were immigrants. Samuel Gompers (1850–1924), the AFL's founder, undertook a massive campaign against socialists and labor opponents of World War I. George Creel, head of the Committee on Public Information (see Note 3 to Part I, Chapter 4) aided him by bankrolling the American Alliance for Labor and Democracy, mainstream labor's answer to the allegedly disloyal socialists.

2. ***John Adams . . . Henry Adams*** John Quincy Adams (1767–1848). President (1825–1829). A man of science and political philosopher of great influence, he lived by the ideal of a government of law rather than of men. Mencken is referring to the book written by Henry Adams (1838–1918), John Quincy's grandson, historian and man of letters, although he has made several errors. The correct title is *The Degradation of the Democratic Dogma*. The introduction Mencken cites was not written by Henry Adams but by his brother, Brooks Adams (1848–1927), and the system proposed was not a weather bureau, but a system of weights and measures. Adams recommended use of the French metric system, which eventually spread across the world. However, at the time "he could find no kindred mind to whom he could confide his perplexities and from whom he could draw a stimulant," his grandson wrote. "In America the work fell dead." John Quincy Adams received "no word of intelligent criticism" for over a decade, and then it was not by an American but from a member of the Royal Engineers in Great Britain.

3. ***What happened in Los Angeles . . . the same circumstances*** Compulsory vaccination in California faced opposition in 1926, including from the Public School Protective League. Many said the health authorities had foisted inoculation through false representation, and that the only goal was profits for doctors. The result was an increase in smallpox cases in Los Angeles, with a conservative estimate of 672 cases and 111 deaths, compared to 478 cases and six deaths in 1925.

4. ***Lloyd-George*** David Lloyd George, 1st Earl of Dwyfor (1863–1945). British prime minister (1916–1922).

5. ***Dr. Hans Delbrück*** (1848–1929). Historian and major figure of Imperial Germany. His scientific study of the military and society stands unchallenged. *Regierung und Volkswille* ("Government and Will of the People") contains the substance of a series of lectures focusing on government, particularly the theory and practice of the German state. His most ambitious work, *History of Warfare in the Framework of Political History*, encompassed four volumes. His method of research and analysis used ancient sources, demography, and economics. He regarded warfare as a cultural feature of societies, subject to evolution and influenced by the economy and political system. Delbrück's criticism of German strategy forced him into an isolated position, but events proved him right, as Imperial Germany went down to defeat.

6. ***Bismarck*** Prince Otto Eduard Leopold von Bismarck (1815–1898). Prussian statesman and first chancellor of the German Empire, to whom Mencken was distantly related. Bismarck was responsible for many social and economic reforms, including workmen's compulsory insurance and the nationalization of industry. He also advocated strong colonial and international policies and protective tariffs.

7. ***Ferdinand Lassalle*** (1825–1864). German socialist. Mencken refers to the time when Germany's political life was paralyzed by Prussian liberal opposition to Bismarck's constitutional changes. Lassalle came forward, calling on workers to concentrate on their political and economic emancipation. Eventually, Lassalle founded an embryo of the German Social Democratric Party.

8. ***Sir Henry Maine*** (1822–1888). English jurist and Cambridge University law professor.

9. ***Stuarts*** The House of Stuart was the first family to rule both England and Scotland (1603 to 1714).

10. ***Lord Mansfield*** William Murray, 1st Earl of Mansfield (1705–1793). British judge and parliamentary debater. His unpopular

defense of Catholics caused a mob to burn his London house during the Gordon Riots.

11. ***Dr. Priestley*** Joseph Priestley (1733–1804). English clergyman and chemist. Co-discoverer of oxygen (See Note 3 to Part III, Chapter 2). Priestley was both conservative and radical. Together with his friend Richard Price he led the Rational Dissenters, who argued problems such as poverty were a consequence of the poor's own folly or lack of education. They were against early welfare programs like the Poor Laws. The working class hated Priestley; he was frequently burned in effigy. But he also supported the French and American Revolutions; his sympathy for the latter provoked a crowd to ransack his home and wreck most of his effects. He later emigrated to America. See http://cepa.newschool.edu/het/profiles/priestley.htm

12. ***anti-vivisection and anti-contraception statutes*** Mencken's interest in medicine and public health prompted him to wage a campaign against anti-vivisectionists in his "The Free Lance" column for the Baltimore *Evening Sun* from 1911 to 1915. "An anti-vivisectionist," he wrote, "is one who strains at a guinea-pig but swallows a baby." His other targets included those who limited free speech by censoring books and plays, closing the mail to "questionable" material, and forbidding any discussion of planned parenthood.

13. ***vox populi*** "Voice of the people" (Latin).

14. ***Lecky*** William Edward Hartpole Lecky (1838–1903). Irish historian, author of *Democracy and Liberty*, which examined modern democracies.

15. ***Wagner*** Mencken is referring to both Richard Wilhelm Wagner (1813–1883), a German composer whose work he considered nothing less than "staggering," and Johannes Peter "Honus" Wagner (1874–1955), one of baseball's greatest players.

16. ***Euripides*** (480-406 BC). Greek playwright; ***Hippocrates*** (ca. 460–ca. 377 BC). Greek physician. He is said to have composed a code of medical ethics. "The Hippocratic oath" is still taken by those entering into the field of medicine; ***Aristotle*** (384-322 BC). Greek philosopher; ***Plato*** (ca 427-347 BC). Greek philosopher.

17. ***Vesalius*** Andreas Vesalius (1514–1564). Belgian anatomist; ***Newton*** Sir Isaac Newton (1642–1727). English natural philosopher and mathematician; ***Bacon*** Roger Bacon (ca. 1214–1294). English philosopher and man of science.

18. ***Abyssinia*** Ethiopia.

19. ***Homer*** (9th or 8th century BC). Greek epic poet; ***Virgil*** (70–19 BC). Roman poet; ***Cervantes*** Miguel de Cervantes (1547–1616). Author of *Don Quijote de la Mancha*; ***Bach*** Johann Sebastian Bach (1685–1750). German composer. Mencken was a great admirer of "the three B's": Bach, Beethoven, and Brahms. He attended many Bach festivals at Bethlehem, Pennsylvania, and enjoyed playing Bach's compositions on his piano; ***Raphael*** (1483–1520). Italian painter; ***Rubens*** Peter Paul Rubens (1577–1640). Flemish painter; ***Beethoven*** Ludwig van Beethoven (1770–1827). German composer of Flemish descent, whose compositions include the *Eroica*, the third of his nine symphonies. "The older I grow," Mencken wrote in his April 24, 1922 "Monday Articles" column for the Baltimore *Evening Sun*, "the more I am convinced that the most portentous phenomenon in the whole history of music was the first public performance of the *Eroica* on April 7, 1805." With this new order of music, Mencken asserted, Beethoven had started "a revolution."

20. ***Hot Dog*** A comedy of the silent film era, released in 1926 and directed by Edgar Kennedy. Another silent comedy short of the same name was released in 1920, written and directed by Fred Hibbard, starring Brownie the Dog.

21. ***The Republic*** A book of philosophy and political theory by Plato.

22. ***Leviathan*** A work of political thought by English philosopher Thomas Hobbes (1588–1679). It focuses on the creation of an ideal state ruled by a sovereign.

23. ***Feinschmecker*** "Connoisseur" (German).

24. ***Egyptian night*** An illusion to Rudyard Kipling's poem "The White Man's Burden." Published in 1899, it was a call to the United States to take up the task of "civilizing" the Philippines following its conquest from Spain. One line warns Americans they will earn "The hate of those ye guard—/The cry of hosts ye humour/(Ah, slowly) toward the light: —/'Why brought ye us from bondage, —/'Our loved Egyptian night?'"

25. ***Chandala*** A Hindu term for a despised or enslaved group. In *The Antichrist*, which Mencken translated, philosopher Friedrich Nietzsche borrowed the term from French writer Louis Jacolliot to describe Judaism and Christianity.

26. ***Latin rite*** Broadly speaking, the Catholic Church.

27. ***Emerson*** Ralph Waldo Emerson (1803–1882). American author, known for his individuality.

28. ***Thoreau*** Henry David Thoreau (1817–1862). American author, famous for *Walden, or Life in the Woods*, his account of simple

living amongst nature, and *Civil Disobedience*, an argument for individual resistance to civic government.

29. ***Clos Vougeot*** One of the largest single vineyards in Burgundy, France, producing "grand cru," considered among the finest red wines in the world.

30. ***mere hatred of beauty*** Mencken expanded on this theme in *Prejudices: Sixth Series* (New York: Knopf, 1927) in an essay on his conviction that certain Americans harbored "a positive libido for the ugly."

31. ***its lack of utilitarian purpose*** As Mencken put it, the final value of an artist's work, "in the open market of the world, is a great deal less than that of a fur overcoat. . . ." From "The Reward of the Artist," published in *Damn! A Book of Calumny* (New York: Philip Goodman, 1918) p. 97).

9. *The Eternal Mob*

1. ***Nero and Torquemada*** Nero Claudius Caesar Drusus Germanicus (AD 37–68). Roman emperor (54–68). His reign's first few years were marked by his wise conduct of public affairs, but his private life was dissipated. He was later accused of starting a fire that burned much of Rome. Nero cruelly persecuted Christians; Tomás de Torquemada, Spanish Inquisitor General. (See Note 4 for Part 1, Chapter 5.)

2. ***Galileo and Savonarola*** Galileo Galilei (1564–1642). Italian physicist and astronomer, considered one of the first modern scientists; Girolamo Savonarola (1452–1498). An Italian Dominican priest and ruler of Florence, famous for his stand against the Church and pleas for social reform. Mencken's parallel does not quite work here as Savonarola is also known for the "Bonfire of the Vanities." In 1497 he ordered items associated with moral laxity—mirrors, cosmetics, poetry, and fine artwork including paintings by Botticelli—burned in a huge pyre. The next year the excommunicated priest was hanged and burned in the same place where the Bonfire was lit.

3. ***Cagliostro*** Alessandro Cagliostro (1743–1795). Italian imposter, traveler, and occultist.

4. ***Danton*** Georges Danton (1759–1794). Leading figure in the early stages of the French Revolution, known for his fiery, passionate speeches and leadership. He played a conspicuous role in the creation of the French Revolutionary Tribunal, an instrument of the Reign of Terror. (See Note 5 to Part I, Chapter 1 and Note 3 to Part III, Chapter 2).

5. ***Barnum*** Phineas Taylor Barnum (1810–1891), American showman, famous for his hoaxes and his circus billed as "The Greatest Show on Earth." It later became the Ringling Brothers and Barnum and Bailey Circus.

6. ***Saturnalia*** Large and public festival of Roman revelry and licentiousness, dedicated to the god Saturn. The Christians used the term to signify an orgy.

7. ***Jahveh*** God (Hebrew).

8. ***Paul*** Saul of Tarsus, also known as Saint Paul the Apostle (AD ca. 3–14 – ca. 62–69). He began his career as a persistent persecutor of Christians. But while on the road to Damascus, he experienced a dramatic conversion and recognized Jesus as the Christ and Son of God. He traveled throughout Asia Minor, Greece, and the Ancient World, preaching the Gospel. Many venerate Paul as an important interpreter of Jesus' teachings but others disagree. Mencken's disparaging view of Paul no doubt stems from his admiration of Thomas Jefferson and Friedrich Nietzsche, who both disputed Paul's teachings. Jefferson was viewed as a heretic when he excised Paul's books from the Bible to return to the true teachings of Christ and the Apostles. Jefferson wrote, "Paul was the first corrupter of the teachings of Jesus." Nietzsche claimed, "God as Paul created him [is] the negation of God."

9. ***Stammvater*** "Staunch supporter" (German).

10. ***Wesley*** John Wesley (1703–1791). English evangelist and father of Methodism.

11. ***Peter*** One of the twelve Apostles chosen among the original disciples of Christ.

12. ***mystical dignity of Rock*** In Matthew 16:18, Jesus tells Peter, "And I also say unto thee, That thou are Peter, and upon this rock I will build my church; and the gates of hell shall not prevail against it." Peter means "rock" in Greek.

13. ***Luther*** Martin Luther (1483–1546). German theologian and leader of the Reformation in Germany

14. ***Calvin*** John Calvin (1509–1564). French theologian, reformer and founder of Calvinism.

II. THE DEMOCRATIC STATE

1. *The Two Kinds of Democracy*

1. ***The notion . . . composed by the folk*** Mencken wrote a very positive review of Louise Pound's *Poetic Origins and the Ballad* in the June 1921 *Smart Set*. Pound asserts that ballads weren't the collec-

tive output of the masses, but works by poets working alone. "The notion that *any* respectable work of art can have a communal origin is wholly nonsensical," Mencken wrote. "The plain people, taking them together, are quite as incapable of a coherent esthetic impulse as they are of courage, honesty or honor."

2. ***Kultur*** "culture" (German).
3. ***ex officio*** "by virtue of one's office" (Latin).
4. ***post hoc*** "after this" (Latin).

2. *The Popular Will*

1. ***von Gottes Gnaden*** "by the Grace of God" (German), a term restricted to monarchs.

2. ***The Merovingian kings*** The Merovingians were a dynasty that ruled parts of France and Germany from the fifth through eighth centuries.

3. ***King John*** John Lackland (1167–1216). King of England from 1199 until his death, he agreed to the Magna Carta (Latin for "Great Charter") on June 15, 1215, at Runnymede, a district near London. Under pressure from rebellious barons, the king pledged, among other things, equal access to the court for all subjects and that the throne would follow the law before imposing punishment. Magna Carta's influence is far-reaching; it is the root of *habeas corpus*, a prisoner's right to be brought before a court in order to determine if his/her imprisonment is lawful.

4. ***Henry VIII*** (1491–1547). King of England from 1509 until his death, Henry VIII is most famous for having eight wives, and executing two of them. Under his rule the Church of England broke with the Papacy.

5. ***Dr. Coolidge*** Calvin Coolidge (1872–1933). Serving as vice president, Coolidge became head of state upon Harding's death in 1923. His administration ran through 1929, a time of great economic growth. Mencken wrote of Coolidge: "There were no thrills while he reigned, but neither were there any headaches. He had no ideas, and he was not a nuisance."

6. ***Bishop Manning*** William Thomas Manning (1866–1949). Episcopal bishop of New York (1921–1946). Manning was in the public eye because of controversies with two of his clergy: the radical Percy Stickney Grant, whose sermons supported labor and socialism, and William Norman Guthrie, whose pagan dances at St.

Mark's-in-the-Bouwerie in New York City went against Manning's notions of propriety.

7. ***The three-class system of voting*** King Frederick Wilhelm IV introduced the Prussian three-class system after the 1848 revolution. Tax revenue divided the three classes: the first was for citizens paying the highest taxes; the second for those paying less; and the third for those contributing little or nothing. The elections were solely for representatives; each class selected a third of the total parliamentarians. The three-class system remained until 1918, when the Weimar Republic was formed.

8. ***Cox . . . antinomian*** James M. Cox (1870–1957). U.S. representative for Ohio (1909–1913), its governor (1913–1915 and 1917–1921), and the badly beaten Democratic 1920 presidential nominee. He divorced his first wife in 1911 and in 1917 remarried.

9. ***that the . . . first wife*** Wilson's first wife, Ellen Louise Axson, died in 1914, leaving him with three daughters. A year later he married Edith Bolling Galt (1872–1961) with whom he had been secretly engaged for several months. The marriage caused consternation among Wilson's advisers, who thought it too soon after Ellen's death.

10. ***Society of the Cincinnati*** A historic association, considered the premier lineage society, with limited and strict membership requirements. It was organized at the American Revolution's end. The first members were many of the time's distinguished military leaders and civil servants, including 23 of the 54 signers of the Constitution.

11. ***Henry Lincoln Johnson*** (1897–1929) African-American World War I hero. Using his rifle and a machete to repel a German attack, he rescued a fellow soldier from capture and saved the lives of his comrades.

12. ***Jacques Loeb*** (1859–1924) German-born American physiologist and biologist. Nominated repeatedly for but never awarded the Nobel Prize, he was the model for Max Gottlieb in Sinclair Lewis's *Arrowsmith.*

13. ***Ku Klux Klan*** A fraternal organization that advocates white supremacy, anti-Semitism, and anti-Catholicism. Founded in 1866 by Confederate army veterans, by 1920 its membership was four million. Throughout his career, Mencken was a strong critic of the Klan. After covering its 1925 parade in Washington, D.C., where 40,000 marched, Mencken was the butt of denunciations by the Knights and Women of the Ku Klux Klan of Little Rock; the Arkansas state senate passed resolutions calling for his deportation.

Mencken argued the "Invisible Empire" was just as "dishonest, ignorant, unjust and cowardly" as the super-patriots who waged the Red Scare.

3. *Disproportional Representation*

1. ***Dred Scott case*** Dred Scott was a slave who sued for his freedom. When his case went before the Supreme Court in 1857, it ruled blacks, even free blacks, could never become U.S. citizens. The decision changed the legal balance in favor of slaveholders. Over time, the Court had to reverse its opinion and admit the decision was unconstitutional. Writing on the Supreme Court's history 70 years later, Chief Justice Charles Evans Hughes observed the Dred Scott case was a "self-inflicted wound" from which the Court took at least a generation to recover.

2. ***Northern Securities case*** Northern Securities Company was a large railroad concern owned by J. P. Morgan and J. D. Rockefeller, among others. Through a large trust, it controlled several railways. This practice had been outlawed since 1890 by the Sherman Anti-Trust Act. President Theodore Roosevelt sued Northern Securities as part of his trust-busting crusade of the early 1900s, which made him popular among the public. The Supreme Court ruled against the company in 1904 and it was dissolved.

3. Mencken shows off his knowledge of medical terms while supplying an appropriate visual image. The ***biceps femoris*** is the muscle of the thigh, situated on the posterior and lateral aspect; the ***semitendinosus*** is situated on the posterior, and the ***semimembranosus*** is situated at the back of the thigh, above and lateral to the *biceps femoris* and *semitendinosus*.

4. ***kine in the byres*** "cows in the barn" (Old Irish).

5. ***as I myself once proposed*** In his "Monday Articles" column for April 11, 1926 ("Lame Ducks"), for the Baltimore *Evening Sun*, Mencken wrote "one of the unpleasant byproducts of the democratic form of Government is that it fills the land with disappointed and embittered men, savagely gnawing their finger nails." The land "swarms" with defeated candidates for the presidency, and the country had to pay the cost for all their "grotesque and indecent wars of revenge." He proposed a Constitutional amendment to get rid of the "soreheads": "On the day his triumphant rival is inaugurated, he shall be hauled to the top of the Washington Monument and there shot, poisoned, stabbed, strangled, and disemboweled and his carcass thrown into the Potomac." There were those who thought Mencken was serious, and bitterly took him to task. He revisits this image of the deadly "sorehead" in pp. 111–114.

6. ***Anti-Saloon League*** A powerful group that lobbied for Prohibition and the abolishment of saloons. It derived most of its support from evangelical Protestant churches, as well as the Women's Christian Temperance Union and the Prohibition Party. The latter was an important force in U.S. politics in the late 19th and early 20th century, and an integral part of the temperance movement.

7. ***Volstead Act*** The National Prohibition Act of 1919, popularly known as the Volstead Act, after its sponsor, U.S. Rep. Andrew John Volstead (1860–1947; R-Minn., 1903–1923). It was passed to provide enforcement for the ratified 18th Amendment. From January 1920 to April 1933, the federal government forbade the manufacture, transport, and sale of alcoholic beverages. Prohibition signaled the triumph of the Fundamentalist movement. For Mencken, it was the ultimate violation of the individual liberties he so cherished. He often wrote about instances where men and women were searched for contraband liquor, and called Prohibition one of the most cynical violations of the Bill of Rights he had ever witnessed. During its 13 years, Mencken devoted at least 42 newspaper articles to Prohibition and made innumerable references to it in his articles, books, and in the pages of the *American Mercury*. When the 18th Amendment was repealed at midnight on April 7, 1933, the spotlight turned to Mencken. Reporters stood to record his opinion of his first legal mug of beer. "Pretty good," he said. "Not bad at all."

8. ***They have already*** Here Mencken's humor is evident, as he exaggerates for effect to make his point.

9. ***Das Kapital . . . Great Gargantua"*** *Das Kapital* is a work by Karl Marx. (See Note 7 to Part 1, Chapter 1.) "The Inestimable Life of the Great Gargantua" is the first part of *Garganta and Pantagruel*, a ribald and satirical fantasy by French author François Rabelais (1494–1553).

10. ***Hans Delbrück*** German historian. See Note 5 for Part I, Chapter 8.

11. ***Hegel*** Georg Wilhelm Friedrich Hegel (1770–1831). German philosopher and creator of "the Absolute," the leading system of metaphysics at the end of the 19th century.

4. *The Politician Under Democracy*

1. ***Professor Robert Michels*** (1876–1936.) German economist and sociologist. He is best known for his book, *Political Parties*, where he writes of the political behavior of intellectual elites. According to his

"iron law of oligarchy," all forms of organization, no matter how democratic, inevitably develop into oligarchies.

2. ***Thersites*** described in Homer's *Iliad* as "the ugliest man that marched on Troy," a fool derided by the Achaean heroes.

3. ***Ulysses*** also known as Odysseus, the king of Ithaca and the central character in Homer's *Odyssey.* Known for his resourcefulness, he remains one of the most influential Greek champions during the Trojan War. His name means "a guide, the one showing the way."

4. ***reductio ad absurdum*** "reduced to absurdity" (Latin).

5. ***Sons of Azrael . . . Order of the Patriarchs Militant*** The Ku Klux Klan divided the country into "Realms" that were headed by "King Kleagles" and "Domains" headed by "Grand Goblins." Over all this ruled the "Imperial Wizard." These names could be related to a particular "Realm" or "Domain" or Mencken may have invented them.

6. ***Homo vulgaris*** Common man (Latin).

5. *Utopia*

1. ***the late Mitchel of New York*** John P. Mitchel (1879–1918). New York City mayor (1914–1917). Mitchel ran for office under an anti-Tammany, reformist ticket: Theodore Roosevelt and Wilson endorsed him. His uncompromising advocacy of military preparedness in World War I, his investigation of religious charities and revelations local police taped telephone lines caused his popularity to drop. He failed to win reelection in 1917.

2. ***the late Lodge of Massachusetts*** Henry Cabot Lodge (1850–1924). Republican congressman (1887–1893) and senator (1893–1924) from Massachusetts. Lodge was a fierce opponent of President Wilson, a Democrat. Lodge faulted Wilson for failing to bolster the military and for what he saw as the president's weak reaction to the sinking of the *Lusitania*. As the Senate Foreign Relations Committee's chairman he led the opposition to the Versailles Treaty and the League of Nations in 1919.

Mencken wrote that "Lodge is above the common level of his party, his country and his race, and he knows it very well, and is not disposed toward the puerile hypocrisy of denying it. He has learning. He has traditions behind him." But Mencken also wondered "what such a man as Lodge thinks secretly of the democracy he processes to cherish. [Lodge could have opted] to set up general practice as a Boston intellectual, groaning and sniffing an easy way through life in the lofty style of the Adams brothers. Instead he dedicated himself to politics, and spent years mastering its complex and yet fundamentally childish technique. . . . A superior fellow? Even so. But superior enough to disdain even the Presidency so fought for by fugitives from the sewers? I rather doubt. My guess is that the gaudy glamour of the White House has intrigued even Henry Cabot—that he would leap for the bauble with the best of them if it were not clearly beyond his reach." (Baltimore *Evening Sun*, June 15, 1920, excerpted in *Chrestomathy*, pages 409 and 410.)

3. ***Penrose*** Sen. Boies Penrose (1860–1921). (R-Pa., 1897–1921). He was identified with high protective tariffs and opposition to Prohibition and women's suffrage. Penrose didn't disguise his cozy relationship with corporations, and was a champion of pro-business legislation. "I believe in the division of labor," he said. "You send us to Congress; we pass laws under which you make money . . . and out of your profits, your further contribute to our campaign funds to bid us back again to pass more laws to enable you to make more money."

4. ***Henry Lincoln Johnson*** African-American World War I hero. See Note 11 to Part II, Chapter 2.

5. ***Westerville, Ohio*** the Anti-Saloon League's headquarters from 1909 to 1948: "the dry capital of America."

6. ***Roosevelt, an imitation aristocrat*** Mencken believed Theodore Roosevelt was not "an aristocrat at all, but a quite typical member of the upper *bourgeoisie*." As he wrote in *Prejudices: Second Series:* "The marks of the thoroughbred were simply not there. The man was blatant, crude, overly confidential, devious, tyrannical, vainglorious, sometimes quite childish." But as Mencken wrote, "the sweet went with the bitter. His disdain of affectation and prudery was magnificent. He hated all pretension save his own pretension . . . His worst defects were the defects of his race and time. Aspiring to be the leader of a nation of third-rate men, he had to stoop to the common level." From "Roosevelt: An Autopsy," *Prejudices: Second Series* (New York: A. A. Knopf, 1920), pages 107–128, excerpted in *Chestomathy*, page 242.)

7. ***Admirable Crichton*** James "the Admirable" Crichton (1560?–1582). Scottish linguist and adventurer.

8. ***Goethe*** Johann Wolfgang von Goethe (1749–1832). German poet.

9. ***Elk*** The Benevolent & Protective Order of Elks, a fraternal, charitable and service order.

10. ***Mayflower*** The steamship *U.S.S. Mayflower* was converted into a luxurious presidential yacht in 1904. It served in that capacity intermittently until 1929.

11. ***Gelehrte*** "scholars" (German).

12. ***Brandeis . . . Anderson*** Louis Dembitz Brandeis (1856–1941), Oliver Wendell Holmes (1841–1935), and Benjamin Nathan Cardozo (1870–1938) were Supreme Court associate justices. In their interpretation of freedom of speech cases, they endeavored for a clearer, more precise distinction between "liberty" and "license." George Weston Anderson (1861–1938) was a respected Boston lawyer, district attorney, and a judge for the First Circuit Court of Appeals. In a widely reported and quoted speech, he said 99% of the pro-German plots never existed and expressed doubts "whether the Red Menace has any more basis in fact than the pro-German peril." Mencken here cites judges he admires, not those who contributed to the anxieties and loss of civil liberties characterizing the years of and after World War I.

13. ***ex cathedra*** "From the chair" (Latin). In Catholicism, it pertains to teaching by authority, e.g., a bishop or the pope. Mencken makes a pun: The judiciary is also known as "the bench."

14. ***The First . . . Fifteenth*** The First Amendment addresses the rights of freedom of religion, assembly, speech and the press. The Second is the right of the people to keep and bear arms. The Fourth guards against unreasonable searches, arrests and seizures of property. The Fifth forbids punishment without due process of law. The Sixth guarantees a speedy public trial for criminal offenses, and right to legal counsel for the accused. The 14th defines U.S. citizenship and citizens' equal protection under the law. The 15th gives the citizen their right to vote, regardless of race, color, or previous condition of servitude.

15. ***F. E. Smith*** Frederick Edwin Smith, 1st Earl of Birkenhead (1872–1930). British Conservative statesman and lawyer. Smith during World War I was in charge of the government's Press Bureau, known for its newspaper censorship. He served as solicitor general, attorney general, and lord chancellor. From the onset of the war, Mencken was dismayed by the "influence of deliberate propaganda" that came to the U.S. through England. Mencken systematically investigated stories that his own newspaper, the *Evening Sun*, had reprinted from the *London Globe*, and found repeated examples of bias and even fraud, guaranteed to influence neutral countries, especially the U.S.

6. *The Occasional Exception*

1. ***Wilhelm I of Prussia*** Mencken is mistaken. It was Frederick Louis Wilhelm IV (1795–1861; king of Prussia 1840–1861) who in

1849 refused the Frankfurt national assembly's offer of the imperial crown; he said he would only accept it from the German princes. It was his brother, William (1797–1888) who ascended to the throne as German emperor in 1871.

2. ***Reich*** empire (German).

3. ***Junker*** The landed aristocracy of Prussia and Eastern Germany. In German it means "young lord," but is understood to mean a country squire, part of the nobility.

4. ***amour propre*** self-respect (French).

5. ***Article II, Sections 1 and 2, of the Constitution*** Article II of the Constitution creates the executive branch. Under Section 1, the president and vice president are elected by the Electoral College, not by popular vote. In Section 2, the president has the power to appoint ambassadors, cabinet officials, and members of the Supreme Court with the "Advice and Consent of the Senate."

6. ***Blease*** Coleman Livingston Blease (1868–1942). Governor of (D, 1911–1915) and senator for (D, 1925–1931) South Carolina. Both a populist and racist, he supported lynching. He was also known for his extravagant gubernatorial pardons.

7. ***Ma Ferguson*** Miriam Amanda Wallace "Ma" Ferguson (1875–1961). Texas' first female governor (D, 1924–1927; and 1933–1935). She opposed the Ku Klux Klan, Prohibition, and foreign language instruction in public schools. The unusual number of pardons during her first term (averaging more than 100 a month) drew accusations of bribes and kickbacks that subsequently led to her defeat.

7. *The Maker of Laws*

1. ***Morley*** John Morley, 1st Viscount of Blackburn (1838–1923). British liberal statesman, writer, and newspaper editor. The sheer force of his honesty and anti-imperialist convictions convinced Mencken that Morley was a man of honor not often seen, let alone elected, in America.

2. ***Eighteenth Amendment*** Prohibition. It was repealed by the 21st Amendment in 1933.

3. ***Roscoe Pound*** (1870–1964). Distinguished legal scholar and dean of Harvard Law School. Pound felt powerless against the hysteria and intolerance of World War I and the Red Scare, and deplored the era's misunderstandings. Once, he complained that "many zealous alumni think that all of my writing is a cover for socialism—and they are exceedingly clamorous."

4. ***Balderdash*** nonsense.

5. ***hedge school*** An old Irish name used in contempt for an inferior institution.

6. ***below the salt*** Of lower rank, signified by where a guest was seated at a long, formal table.

7. ***dummy*** an imaginary person

8. ***Knights of Zoroaster*** The Independent Knights of Zoroaster, a secretive Fort Wayne, Indiana, fireman's club of the 1870s and 1880s.

9. ***Two of the most . . . snob of the Upper House*** The 69th Congress ran from 1925 through 1926. The senators, both Republicans, were George Wharton Pepper (1867–1961), serving from 1922 to 1927; and David Aiken Reed (1880–1953), serving from 1922 to 1935, nicknamed "the most tactless member of both houses of Congress." A cursory review of Reed's career reveals no obvious "dizzy flops." Pepper's "flop" may be his support in late 1925 of President Coolidge's strategy for the U.S. role in the Permanent Court of International Justice, after Coolidge rejected Pepper's plan for the World Court a year earlier. Pepper was Lodge's successor as the Senate's "intellectual snob." Like the Bostonian, he was an author and a scholar.

10. ***Reed of Missouri*** Sen. James Alexander Reed (1861–1944; D-Mo., 1911–1929). Reed opposed to the League of Nations and assailed Wilson's leadership, refusing to campaign on behalf of pro-League candidates in the 1920 election. Wilson personally involved himself in the effort "to rid Democracy of Reed." In an overwhelming upset, Reed beat the president's handpicked candidate. Mencken admired Reed for years, and wrote a moving tribute to him in the April 1929 *American Mercury*. Reed not only thrived on controversy: He was a skillful orator, as Mencken demonstrates in this *Congressional Record* citation. Mencken's admiration of Reed was so great he persuaded him to contribute an essay to the *Mercury*. Reed was a lawyer, and during the "Hatrack" case of 1926 he offered his services to Mencken *pro bono*. He also authored one of the bills to change the Post Office's censorship powers.

11. ***This is what he said . . . On June 2, 1924*** An avid reader of *The Congressional Record*, Mencken was always thrilled to encounter oratory at its best, and this is no exception. On June 2, 1924, Congress attempted to pass a constitutional amendment that would authorize a national child labor law. Although Reed was against child labor, he maintained the amendment was faulty, with little regard for the conse-

quences. He argued it took from several states the right to control the hours and conditions of every citizen under 18, that it deprived parents the right to control their children, and concentrated all the powers in Congress. By way of example, Reed cited the possibility that a 17-year-old could be unfairly arrested for working at the family farm. In the end, the amendment was dropped. In 1938, the Fair Labor Standards Act was passed, placing limits on forms of child labor.

8. *The Rewards of Virtue*

1. ***Katzenjammer*** "commotion" (German).

2. ***Whiskey Ring*** Exposed in 1875, the Whiskey Ring was a conspiracy of mostly Republican politicians to defraud the federal government of more than $3 million in taxes. The scheme involved an extensive network of bribes involving government agents, whiskey distillers, and distributors, and led many to believe that it was part of a plot to finance the Republican Party by fraud. During the 1920s, the Anti-Saloon League used examples of the Whiskey Ring as propaganda to show that drink was "the Great Destroyer." (See also Note 11 to Part III, Chapter 4.)

3. ***Beer Trust*** In 1898, 17 of the 21 Baltimore-area breweries merged into the Maryland Brewing Company, a "beer trust." See Burt Solomon, *Where They Ain't: The Fabled Life and Untimely Death of the Original Baltimore Orioles, the Team that Gave Birth to Modern Baseball* (New York: Free Press, 1999), pp. 142–143.

4. ***the anti-Saloon League . . . corruption*** In 1919 the Anti-Saloon League stood at the peak of its power, but corruption threatened to unravel it. One former superintendent from St. Louis had abandoned the League, accusing its members of everything from larceny to rape. Another from Washington State was charged with stealing church collections and fleeing with them to Alaska. U.S. Rep. Jefferson "Jeff" McLemore (1857–1929; D-Texas, 1915–1918) said the League was "an unspeakable fraud" of gross corruption. He cited a case of 19 preachers from its Michigan organization, whose adultery, perjury, blackmail, bigamy, swindling, and licentious assaults on a small boy yielded prison sentences for two and church expulsion for six. One of the most nefarious of cases involved Mencken's old friend, William H. Anderson (1874–1961?). While serving as the League's New York state chief, he was found guilty of forgery and served nine months in prison. Despite the League's corruption, Wayne Bidwell Wheeler (1869–1927), its attorney and *de facto* leader, wielded enormous influence and power. By

1926 some on Capitol Hill were questioning the League's spending in congressional races.

5. ***When, fifteen or twenty years ago*** Mencken refers to pieces he wrote for his "The Free Lance" column from 1911 to 1915.

6. ***Mayo brothers*** William James Mayo (1861–1939) and Charles Horace Mayo (1865–1939), both physicians and co-founders of the Mayo Clinic in Rochester, Minnesota. It is regarded one of the world's foremost medical treatment and research institutions.

7. ***Dr. George Crile*** (1864–1943) Recognized as the first American surgeon to perform successfully a direct blood transfusion and for his pioneering work in improving anaesthetic methods.

8. ***faculty of the Johns Hopkins*** the doctors practicing at Johns Hopkins Hospital in Baltimore, many of whom were friends of Mencken.

9. ***The comstocks . . . on that charge*** Anthony Comstock (1844–1915), a U.S. Postal Inspector and politician. Comstock founded the New York Society for the Suppression of Vice, an institution zealously dedicated to supervising public morality. In 1873 he convinced Congress to pass the Comstock Law, which made illegal the delivery or transportation of "obscene, lewd or lascivious" material or information. "Comstocks" were men who, like their namesake, sought to censor whatever they deemed as indecent.

In April 1926 the *American Mercury* was banned from mail delivery because of an innocuous but true story about a prostitute named "Hatrack." Mencken sued to regain postal access. He risked imprisonment by challenging the Comstock Law. The "Hatrack case" was recognized as a landmark suit against censorship. For a decade thereafter, no such trial would take place in the U.S. without some reference to the *Mercury*. Mencken's name would become internationally identified with freedom of speech.

10. ***Fremont Older*** (1856–1935). Editor of the *San Francisco Chronicle, San Francisco Call*, and *San Francisco Bulletin*. He is remembered as one of the most dynamic crusading newspapermen in the 20th century's first half. He fought against corruption and for civil rights, famously defending the radical labor leader, Thomas Joseph Mooney (1882–1942), who was charged with the Preparedness Day Parade bombing of 1916.

11. ***Julian Harris*** (1874–1963). Owner and editor of the *Columbus Enquirer Sun* (Georgia). Mencken admired Harris's fights on behalf of religious freedom and racial tolerance. His paper won the Pulitzer Prize for public service in 1926 in its struggle against the Klan.

12. ***Emile Faguet*** (1847–1916). French writer and critic, known for his work on political liberty.

9. *Footnote on Lame Ducks*

1. ***This Majestic Victim . . . Burr . . . Bryan*** All of the below were failed presidential candidates. Here "majestic victim" means "glorified loser."

Burr Aaron Burr (1756–1836). American Revolutionary War officer, senator from New York (1791–1797), and vice president to Thomas Jefferson (1801–1805). He mortally wounded Alexander Hamilton (1755–1804), the founder of the Federalist Party, in a duel. Burr later formed an unsuccessful plot to start a new nation in the western frontier.

Clay Henry Clay (1777–1852). Senator (1806–1807; 1810–1811; 1831–1842; and 1849–1852) and congressman (1811–1814; 1815–1821; 1823–1825) for Kentucky; secretary of state under John Quincy Adams (1825–1829); and six-time House speaker.

Calhoun John Caldwell Calhoun (1782–1850). Congressman (1811–1817) and senator (1832–1843, and 1845–1850) for South Carolina; secretary of war (1817–1825); and vice-president (1825–1832). He advocated the "Theory of Nullification": the right of a state to nullify or invalidate any federal law it deems unconstitutional. Calhoun argued for the states' right to secede from the Union. This was put to a test in 1832, after Calhoun's home state of South Carolina passed an ordinance to nullify federal tariffs. Calhoun resigned as vice president and accepted election to the Senate. There he continued to proclaim slavery was a necessary good, not an evil.

Douglas Stephen Arnold Douglas (1813–1861). Democratic congressman (1843–1847) and senator (1847–1861) from Illinois. Douglas was one of the most important congressional leaders during the 1850s. He authored the Kansas-Nebraska Act of 1854 to respond to the slavery question. Douglas failed to win the Democratic presidential nomination in 1852 and 1856. His Republican opponent in his 1858 senatorial reelection campaign was Abraham Lincoln; Douglas defeated Lincoln. Their debates throughout Illinois on slavery are famous. Douglas faced Lincoln again in the 1860 presidential election. While Douglas won the party's nomination, his uncompromising stance on slavery prompted the Democrats' southern faction to forward its own candidate. This split helped Lincoln win the election.

Blaine James Gillespie Blaine (1830–1893). Republican congressman (1863–1876) and senator (1876- 1881) from Maine. Known for his aggressive nature, this three-time House speaker played a leading role in framing the Reconstruction's tempestuous politics. His 1884 presidential run featured an enormous amount of personal acrimony. Refusing to be a presidential candidate again, he served twice as secretary of state.

Greeley Horace Greeley (1811–1872). The *New York Tribune's* editor and a founder of the Republican Party. He played an indirect role in Lincoln winning the 1860 Republican presidential candidacy. Greeley may have aspired to hold considerable sway over the new president. However, such power never came to pass. During the Civil War he argued for letting the South "go in peace." Greeley's alliance with the Radical Republicans and his lobbying for a quick end to the war annoyed Lincoln. After the war he was a harsh critic of President Andrew Johnson and advocated for his impeachment. His antagonism toward the White House persisted when Ulysses S. Grant took office. He was the presidential candidate in 1872 for both the new Liberal Republican Party and the Democrats but lost in a landslide against Grant.

Frémont John C. Frémont (1813–1890). Military officer and explorer. He was both the first Republican presidential candidate and the first to run on anti-slavery platform. While serving as Lincoln's commander of "the Department of the West," Frémont took it upon himself to author an order ending slavery in Missouri and institute martial law. Lincoln, distressed by this presumptuous move and other blunders by Frémont, removed him from command. But Frémont remained in good standing with the Radical Republicans. He briefly ran as their presidential candidate in 1864 but eventually withdrew his nomination.

For Roosevelt and Bryan, see Note 3 for Part 1, Chapter 4.

2. ***1840*** Mencken is mistaken about Clay's third attempt at the presidency: Clay ran for president as a Whig in 1844, not 1840.

3. ***Mellons, Morgans and Charlie Schwabs*** Three of the richest men of Mencken's time: Andrew W. Mellon (1855–1937), banker, industrialist, and philanthropist; John Pierpont Morgan (1837–1913), financier and banker; and Charles Michael Schwab (1862–1939), steel industry magnate.

4. ***Jackson*** Andrew Jackson (1767–1845), president (1829–1837) and co-founder of the Democratic Party. (See Note 6 to Part I, Chapter 1.)

5. ***Blennerhassett*** Harman Blennerhassett (1765–1831). An Irish-American lawyer who became involved in Aaron Burr's conspiracy

to form a new nation in the western frontier. He helped furnish funds and lent his island on the Ohio River as a rendezvous point. When the plans collapsed Blennerhassett was arrested and imprisoned.

6. ***Hancock*** Winfield Scott Hancock (1824–1886). Civil War Union general. During Reconstruction in Louisiana he renewed civil jurisdiction and declined to use military power to help Radical Republicans. This perturbed Ulysses S. Grant, his superior. Grant sent Hancock to New York City, and later, when Grant won the presidency, to the Department of Dakota. Going back as far as 1864 Democrats had eyed Hancock as a possible presidential contender. A Civil War hero, his record could counter Republicans' "Bloody Shirt" rhetoric. Hancock won the Democratic presidential nomination in 1880. Both he and his Republican opponent, James A. Garfield, underwhelmed voters. The race was close, and in the end Hancock lost due to the betrayal of New York's Tammany Democrats, who cast their electoral votes with Garfield.

7. ***the bloody shirt*** Ben F. Butler, a U.S. representative from Massachusetts, shook on the floor of Congress the bloodstained pajama shirt of a carpetbagger flogged by Klansmen. During the Reconstruction, "Bloody Shirt" was a byword for the Republican propaganda tactic of reminding voters of the South's disloyalty.

8. ***his débâcle in 1912*** While in office Roosevelt endorsed his secretary of war, William H. Taft (1857–1930) for the 1908 Republican presidential nomination, believing Taft would continue with his policies. Taft won the election, and Roosevelt said he'd never run again for president. But by 1912 he changed his mind. After losing to Taft at the Republican convention, Roosevelt became the Progressive Party's "Bull Moose" candidate. In the end Wilson trounced both Roosevelt and Taft, carrying 40 out of 48 states.

9. ***German scheme of things*** After Mencken wrote of "Roosevelt's philosophical kinship to the Kaiser" he "received letters of denunciations from all parts of the United States, and not a few forthright demands" that he "recant on penalty of lynch law." Mencken also pointed to Nietzsche's influence on Roosevelt's thinking. See "Roosevelt: An Autopsy," *Prejudices: Second Series* (New York: Alfred A. Knopf, 1920), excerpted in *Chestomathy*, pp. 230-232.

10. ***Clarence Darrow's cross-examination*** See Notes 6 and 7 to Part I, Chapter 4.

11. ***1600 Pennsylvania avenue, N.W.*** The White House's address.

12. ***Sherman's army*** Union General William Tecumseh Sherman (1820–1891) in November 1864 began his "March to the Sea," culminating in the fall of Savannah a month later. His "scorched earth" policy was notorious. His troops ransacked and destroyed railroads, farms and homes.

13. ***tertiary lues*** another name for syphilis.

14. ***maison de santé*** "hospital" (French).

15. ***ladies of the half and quarter worlds*** Mencken's polite reference to whores.

III. DEMOCRACY AND LIBERTY

1. *The Will to Peace*

1. ***Homo vulgaris*** "Common man" (Latin).

2. ***Wilson, Palmer, Burleson*** Mencken lumps Wilson in the same breath as the other two gentlemen. Mencken felt that Wilson's neutrality of 1914–1917 was hypocritical and entirely false. Rather than viewing Wilson as a great moral statesman, Mencken called him "a Christian cad," and felt the excesses of the Espionage Act bore him out.

Alexander Mitchell Palmer (1872–1936). U.S. attorney general from 1919 to 1921. His controversial "Palmer Raids" yielded the arrest of at least 10,000 suspected subversives.

Albert Sidney Burleson (1863–1937). U.S. postmaster general (1913–1921). He instituted racist policies and banned postal employees from striking. During World War I he enthusiastically upheld the Espionage Act by reviewing suspicious material forwarded to him by subordinates. Anti-war literature was closed to postal delivery.

3. ***Nietzsche*** Friedrich Wilhelm Nietzsche (1844–1900). Highly influential German philosopher, most famous for his theory of the "übermensch" ("superman"). Mencken's book, *The Philosophy of Friedrich Nietzsche*, is said to have contributed more to the popular understanding of the philosopher than any other American work. In 1920 Mencken translated and wrote an introduction to Nietzsche's *The Antichrist.*

4. ***Schopenhauer*** Arthur Schopenhauer (1788–1860). German philosopher, known for his pessimistic view that regarded life as futile.

5. ***Emersonian counsel*** See Note 27 for Part I, Chapter 8. Emerson encouraged individualism in *Essays: First Series* and *The Conduct of Life*.

6. ***droit de seigneur*** "right of the first night" (French); a feudal lord's prerogative to deflower a subject's bride.

7. ***lex de majestate*** "the law of the land" (Latin)

8. ***Saturninus*** Lucius Appuleius Saturninus (d. 100 B.C.) Roman tribune and mob-master.

9. ***pulls his forelock*** obsequiously salutes.

10. ***Huxley*** Thomas Henry Huxley (1825–1895). English biologist who defended Charles Darwin's theory of evolution. He also popularized science, and invented the word "agnosticism" to describe the view that God's existence is inherently unknowable. Mencken credited Huxley for giving order to his ideas and being a major influence on his writing.

11. ***Harding, jabbering of normalcy*** Warren Harding (1865–1923). President (R, 1921–1923). When Harding pledged a retreat back to simpler times—normality—he unintentionally coined a new word. His promise of a "return to normalcy" reflected three postwar trends: renewed isolationism; the resurgence of nativism; and a turning away from the government activism prevalent in the Progressive Era. After hearing Harding's inaugural address, Mencken wrote it was "the worst English that I have ever encountered."

12. ***Tabakparlement*** Literally, "tobacco parliament" (German). Possibly a reference to Frederick II, King of Prussia, and his habit of convening clubby, smoke-filled meetings.

13. ***Pershing*** John Joseph Pershing (1860–1948). General. Pershing in 1916 led an expedition to find Pancho Villa after his attack on Columbus, New Mexico. (See Note 2 to Part I, Chapter 4.) When America entered World War I the following year, he headed U.S. forces.

2. *The Democrat as Moralist*

1. ***Flavius Honorius*** (AD 384-423). Emperor of Rome's western sphere. A weak ruler, his reign saw revolts and barbarian invasions, including the sack of Rome in 410.

2. ***Charlemagne*** Charles the Great (AD 742–814). Regarded as Europe's founder. He was a patron of literature, science and art, and strengthened Christianity on the Continent.

3. ***Lavoisier*** Antoine-Laurent de Lavoisier (1743–1794). French nobleman known as "the father of modern chemistry." He co-discovered and named oxygen (see Note 11 to Part I, Chapter 8), devised the first table of elements, and was part of a team that developed the metric system. During the Reign of Terror, Jean-Paul Marat, a firebrand of the French Revolution who was barred from joining the Academy of Sciences by Lavoisier, accused him of imprisoning Paris and blocking its air cir-

culation through a wall he constructed around the capital. Lavoisier was tried and executed. "The Republic has no need of scientists," replied the judge at his trial to an appeal to spare his life.

4. ***Louis XVI*** See Note 5 for Part I, Chapter 1.

5. ***Wat Tyler*** Walter Tyler (?–1381). Leader of the English Peasant's Revolt of 1381, commonly known as Wat Tyler. There is some speculation on how the quick-witted Tyler established discipline among the mob, but scholars agree one method was the execution of thieves among his followers. His authority never seems to have been questioned by any rival. A crowd of 20,000 assembled as Tyler went alone to speak to King Richard II to relate the peasants' grievances. Some sources say Tyler was unarmed; others say he approached the king with a dagger in his hand. At that moment, William Walworth, the mayor of London, struck Tyler, and one of the king's squires slashed him with a sword. The rebellion ended shortly after Tyler's death.

6. ***Good Man*** An allusion to "*bonhomme*." Literally "good man," the French word's etymology traces back to the 12th and 13th centuries when it meant a simple, kind peasant. See *Le Grand Robert de Langue Française*, Volume 1 (Paris: Directionnaires Le Robert, 2001). Nietzsche commented on the "good man" concept: "[T]he good human being has to be *undangerous* in the slaves' way of thinking: he is good-natured, easy to deceive, a little stupid perhaps, *un bonhomme*." (Italics Nietzsche's.) See Friedrich Nietzsche, *Beyond Good and Evil*, trans. Walter Kaufmann (New York: Vintage Books, 1966), page 207.

7. ***comstockery*** A noun coined by playwright George Bernard Shaw (1856–1950) after his work was censored in America: "censorship because of perceived obscenity or immorality" without regard for culture or merit. "Comstockery is the world's standing joke at the expense of the United States," he said. "Europe likes to hear of such things. It confirms the deep-seated conviction of the Old World that America is a provincial place, a second-rate country-town civilization after all." See Note 9 for Part II, Chapter 8 for Anthony Comstock and "comstocks".

8. ***John Milton*** (1608–1674). English poet, best known for *Paradise Lost.*

9. ***"The Pilgrim's Progress"*** a prose allegory by Christian writer and teacher John Bunyan (1628–1688), one of the most widely read books in the English language.

10. ***Code Napoléon*** The Napoleonic Code, originally called the Code civil des Français, passed in 1804. It was named after Napoleon,

who played a role in its devising. It encompasses all of French law as outlined in five codes passed in the early 19th century. Before the Code Napoléon, France's law varied regionally, with the north following customary, Germanic law and the south and east adhering to Roman law. The Code brought uniformity to the nation's legal system.

11. ***The Fathers were . . . the democratic scheme*** The Constitution initially specified that U.S. senators were to be elected by state legislators. Under the 17th Amendment, adopted in 1913, voters directly elect their state's two senators.

12. ***The grotesque anti-syndicalist . . . and Indiana are typical*** The anti-syndicalism laws appealed to public opinion by striking at Bolshevism and other radical ideologies. Most of them were enacted during the tension of 1919, although in some states they continued into the 1920s. One prominent anti-syndicalism case in California involved Charlotte Anita Whitney (1867–1955), a well-known philanthropist and social worker. She joined the Socialist Party after hearing the charismatic speeches of labor leader Eugene Debs. She opposed U.S. involvement in World War I and fought for the free speech rights of the Industrial Workers of the World, a radical union. When Whitney and other socialists formed the more radical Communist Labor Party she was arrested in 1919 for sedition under the state's Criminal Syndicalism Act, wartime legislation barring opposition to the draft and other "disloyal speech." After a dubious trial, during which her attorney died but no postponement was permitted, she was sentenced to 14 years in prison. Her fight for civil liberties prompted the Baltimore *Sun* to declare in an editorial that there was something "obviously rotten" with the state of California. It wasn't until 1971 that the Criminal Syndicalism Act was declared unconstitutional. (See http://www.aclu-sc.org/About/History/1923.)

Mississippi passed its anti-evolution statute in early 1926. Unlike in Tennessee, the ACLU could not entice a local teacher to challenge it. Its anti-evolution statute was finally repealed in 1967.

The Anti-Saloon League's activities in Ohio provided a microcosm of its work nationwide. The temperance issue had raged in Ohio decades before the Anti-Saloon League's appearance, and by Prohibition its laws were strict. But the heaviest penalty for the violation of Prohibition in 1925 in was in Indiana. There the average jail sentence for possession of liquor was 185 days, and the average fine $525. By comparison, Louisiana had a jail sentence of five days and an $86 fine; New York had no jail sentence and a fine of $24. Indiana law was so strict that Gary's mayor in March 1923 was fined $2,000 and sent to prison for 18 months for the sale and transportation of liquor.

13. ***Thaw*** Henry Kendall Thaw (1871–1947). A Pittsburgh coal and steel baron's son and an actress's jealous husband. Thaw shot and killed architect Stanford White (1853–1906) and claimed it was to save his young wife, the actress Evelyn Nesbit, from the elderly man's attentions. More than a score of trials and legal proceedings began in 1907, ending 17 years later. The case showed how atonement might be averted by a murderer with deep pockets.

14. ***Fatty Arbuckle*** Roscoe Conkling Arbuckle (1887–1933). One of the most popular American silent film comedians of the 1920s. Nicknamed "Fatty" for of his rotund figure, in 1921 he was accused of raping an actress with a champagne bottle and crushing her with his weight, causing her to die of a ruptured bladder. The scandal rocked Hollywood. Tabloids portrayed Arbuckle as a pervert. His films were withdrawn from distribution and he was fired from Paramount Studio. Calls for reform led to the Production Code's creation, which set decency standards in all Hollywood films. Although Arbuckle was cleared of all allegations, the infamy surrounding him destroyed his career and personal life.

15. ***The Prohibitionists . . . war hysteria*** German-Americans opposed Prohibition. They felt the Anti-Saloon League and Prohibition Party were attacking their customs and heritage. This was not paranoia. "The prohibitionists might never have been able to gain the necessary vote in the Senate and House of Representatives to gain the passage of the Eighteenth Amendment if they had not had a murderous stroke of luck," observed historian Andrew Sinclair in his book *Prohibition: the Era of Excess* (Boston: Little, Brown, 1962). "Their chance was the Great War. . . . Pabst and Busch were German, therefore beer was unpatriotic. Liquor stopped American soldiers from firing straight; therefore liquor was a total evil. Brewing used up eleven million loaves of barley bread a day, which could have fed the starving Allies; therefore the consumption of alcohol was treason. Pretzels were German in name; therefore to defend Old Glory, they were banned from the saloons of Cincinnati." In rapid succession laws were enacted that expanded the government's power beyond anything seen in peacetime. By 1925 arrests by federal officials numbered 62,747 and there were 50,723 prosecutions in court.

16. ***William Graham Sumner*** (1840–1910), social scientist and educator. Sumner, a social Darwinist, claimed the distinction of wealth

and status among men was the direct result of inherently different capacities. He decried any and all egalitarian movements that sought to uplift the downtrodden at the ordinary middle-class citizen's expense. In an 1883 lecture he dubbed this ignored, self-sufficient individual "the Forgotten Man." When President Franklin Delano Roosevelt (1882–1945; D, 1933–1945) used "the Forgotten Man" in speeches pushing his New Deal policies, it infuriated Mencken, who saw it as a blatant misuse of Sumner's term.

3. *Where Puritanism Fails*

1. ***California and Pennsylvania*** The American Legion pressed successfully for the arrest and conviction of those it deemed guilty of seditious speech in states including Kansas, Idaho, and Minnesota. In California, it determined radicals could be immediately incarcerated or deported. The situation in the Pennsylvania coal and iron districts in 1919 and 1920 was no less grim. The rights of free speech and free assemblage were broken down by a series of local ordinances. Newspapers were rigidly controlled as well. Civil liberties were denied to such a degree that most were too intimidated to protest. Ironically, suspicion of outside agitators was so great that when Wilson's Committee on Public Information (see Note 3 for Part I, Chapter 4) sent a speaker to give a patriotic speech on Abraham Lincoln he was arrested and jailed for three days.

2. ***Polizei*** "police" (German).

3. ***Bill of Rights*** From 1918 to 1926 the press was filled with stories of brutal police attacks on Pennsylvania labor unions that were fighting for their First Amendment rights. Arthur Garfield Hays, the ACLU lawyer, repeatedly spoke out against the assault, battery and false arrests. "The average legislator today knows as much about the fundamentals of the Constitution and the Bill of Rights as a Fiji Islander knows about Sanskrit," remarked a former Kentucky governor.

4. ***There are many statutes . . . unpopular thoughts*** See Note 12 for Part III, Chapter 2 on California's anti-syndicalism laws and Charlotte Anita Whitney.

5. ***ipso facto*** "the fact by itself" (Latin). By the case's very nature.

6. ***". . . of free speech."*** In his "Monday Articles" column for February 8, 1926 ("Liberty with Reservations"), for the Baltimore *Evening Sun*, Mencken wrote of the Reverend Luther B. Wilson's speech at the Cathedral of St. John the Divine in New York. Wilson, a

bishop of the Methodist Episcopal Church in Baltimore, proposed atheists should be seen as traitors, and consequently charged with treason.

7. ***Arthur Garfield Hays*** (1881–1954). Lawyer of German-Jewish descent and counsel for the ACLU. He was involved in many notable civil liberty struggles of his day, including the Sacco and Vanzetti case and the Scopes trial. Hays represented Mencken when he was arrested in Boston in 1926 for selling a banned copy of the *American Mercury*, an incident that set off the "Hatrack" case.

8. ***Stewart*** Arthur Thomas Stewart, prosecutor for the Scopes trial. See Note 7 for Part I, Chapter 5.

9. ***Raulston*** At the Scopes trial Mencken observed how Judge Raulston favored the prosecution. "The judge let it stand in the record," Mencken wrote, "where it remains for the instruction of posterity."

10. ***I do not . . . intellectual resilience.*** In an essay in the May 1922 *Smart Set,* Mencken mused on the science of penology. When considering a jury or a judge, he wrote "[w]hat we find practically is a crowd of poltroons in the jury box venting their envious hatred of enterprise and daring upon a man who, at worst, is at least as decent as they are; and a scoundrel on the bench lording it over a scoundrel on the dock because the latter is less clever than he is." The Scopes trial jury was composed of middle-aged farmers, Fundamentalists with little formal education. Evolution was not only foreign to their way of thinking but also a challenge to their beliefs. "Such a jury," Mencken wrote in the Baltimore *Evening Sun* on July 11, 1925, "in a legal sense, may be fair, but it would certainly be spitting in the eye of reason to call it impartial." The Pittsburgh *Courier,* an African-American newspaper, said the jury was the same type that black men and women faced in Southern courtrooms every day.

11. ***Russian gold*** In order to underwrite the purchase of western technology, the Bolsheviks in the early 1920s sold Russian gold overseas. See J.D. Smele, "White gold: the Imperial Russian Gold Reserve in the anti-Bolshevik east, 1918–?—An unconcluded chapter in the history of the Russian Civil War," *Europe-Asia Studies*, December 1994.

12. ***Debs*** Eugene Victor Debs (1855–1926). American socialist leader and founder of the Social Democratic Party. While Mencken rejected socialism on principle, he opposed Debs's imprisonment. Debs was arrested under the Espionage Act for an anti-war speech in

1918. The Supreme Court ruled against his appeal and he went to prison. He was finally released in late 1921. In the January 1922 *Smart Set* Mencken called his arrest a "plain violation of his constitutional rights."

4. *Corruption Under Democracy*

1. ***cult of Service*** See Note 9 to Part I, Chapter 5.

2. ***wood alcohol*** methanol, the simplest form of alcohol, used as anti-freeze or fuel.

3. ***war to end war*** World War I.

4. ***Tocqueville*** Count Alexis de Tocqueville (1805–1859). French historian whose best known work, *Democracy in America,* is considered the first impartial and systematic study of American institutions.

5. ***the Adams Brothers*** Brooks Adams (1848–1927) and his brother, Henry Adams (1838–1918), both historians and grandsons of John Quincy Adams, exchanged a series of letters in which they developed the then-revolutionary idea that American democracy was foredoomed to degradation and decay. Henry completed his memoirs, *The Education of Henry Adams*, in 1905, but it was not widely published until his death in 1918. It won the Pulitzer Prize for autobiography the following year. The book was a sharp critique of the changing political, intellectual, and technological fronts of his lifetime.

6. ***Wilfrid Scawen Blunt*** (1840–1922). English author, diplomat and explorer. His opposition to British imperialism and exploitation made him the victim of imprisonment and censorship.

7. ***Friedrich von Gentz*** (1764–1832) German journalist and statesman.

8. ***Metternich*** Prince Klemens Metternich (1773–1859). Austrian politician and statesman.

9. ***Third Republic*** The Third Republic (1870–1940) saw many controversies, including the Panama Scandal of 1889 that involved government officials charged with corruption and bribery. But the Republic's most famous scandal was the Dreyfus Affair. In 1893 Captain Alfred Dreyfus was accused of selling military secrets to Germany. He was convicted of treason and sentenced to life in prison. The scandal divided France. Dreyfus was Jewish, and his case unleashed a storm of anti-Semitism. Novelist Émile Zola (1840–1902) and statesman and journalist Georges Clemenceau (1841–1929) took up Dreyfus' cause. He was exonerated in 1906.

10. ***German Republic*** Germany's change to a parliamentary democracy was carried through during the last few months of 1918 but its new constitution was not established until late 1919.

11. ***Grant*** Ulysses S. Grant (1822–1885). Civil War general and president (R, 1869–1877). His presidency was rocked by scandals, among them Black Friday, a financial crisis set off by Wall Street speculators in 1869; several Grant administration insiders were involved. But the most famous scandal was the Whiskey Ring of 1875, in which over $3 million in federal taxes was stolen with the aid of White House officials, including Orville E. Babcock (1835–1884), Grant's private secretary, and William W. Belknap (1829–1890), secretary of war. Although there is no evidence that Grant profited from his subordinates' corruption, he did not take a firm stand, even after their guilt was established.

12. ***Marconi scandal*** A British political controversy of 1912. It revolved around supposed insider trading of the stock of Marconi Company, the world's first radio producer, by persons close to the government.

13. ***raids . . . the Wilson administration*** According to historian William E. Leuchtenburg, in 1914 the United States was in debt by $3 billion. By 1919 it had loaned over $10 billion to other nations to carry on World War I as well as to pay for postwar reconstruction. See William E. Leuchtenburg, *The Perils of Prosperity 1914-32* (The University of Chicago Press, 1958), p. 108.

14. ***deliberate thievings . . . Harding*** Harding appointed many of his allies from his home state to prominent positions. Among the "Ohio Gang" was Harry M. Daugherty (1860–1941), a Republican boss who engineered Harding's nomination, later appointed as attorney general. Kickbacks, bribes, and underground drug and alcohol distribution were just a few of the gang's crimes. The time's most notorious controversy was the Teapot Dome Scandal. Albert B. Fall (1861–1944), secretary of the interior, was convicted of accepting bribes and personal loans in exchange for leasing public oil fields to private businesses. Nothing indicates Harding knew about the crimes that transpired during his administration.

15. ***I have exhibited . . . the common good*** Mencken refers to his essay "The Husbandman" in *Prejudices: Fourth Series* (New York: Alfred A. Knopf, 1924), where he disputes the theory that farmers need economic assistance. "When the going is good for him he robs the rest

of us up to the extreme limit of our endurance; when the going is bad he comes bawling for help out of the public till."

16. ***Fourteen Points*** Wilson's idealistic goals for peace presented to Congress in January 1918. The Fourteen Points became the basis for Germany's terms of surrender as negotiated in the Paris Peace Conference of 1919 and documented in the Treaty of Versailles, but only four of them were completely adopted. The British were against freedom of the seas, and the French demanded reparations. Wilson was forced to compromise to ensure that his most important point, the League of Nations, was adopted. The Treaty of Versailles caused great bitterness in Germany and triggered the rise of the Third Reich in the 1930s.

17. ***a helpless foe*** Germany.

18. ***League of Nations*** Formed after World War I, the League of Nations was an international organization dedicated to worldwide cooperation, peace, and welfare. Although Wilson had been the driving force behind the League, the Senate voted against U.S. participation, reflecting its isolationist mood. This weakened much of the League's potential power. While it was able to settle a few minor disputes, the League failed miserably in its goal of preventing aggression, as World War II made clear. It was replaced by the United Nations in 1945.

19. ***Lecky*** See Note 14 to Part I, Chapter 8.

20. ***perfide Albion*** "treacherous Britain" (French).

21. ***two houses of Congress*** After Sen. Robert M. La Follette (1855–1925, R-Wis., 1906–1925) introduced a resolution in 1921 for an investigation into the Teapot Dome scandal, his office was broken into and his files ransacked. Three years later, testifying before a Senate committee, a former Justice Department agent confessed to the break-in. He said two other legislators, also Harding critics, were examined.

22. ***Mill*** John Stuart Mill (1806–1873). English philosopher and political economist. In *On Liberty*, he explores the nature and limits of power society can legitimately exercise over the individual.

23. ***Brooks Adams*** (1848–1927). See Note 2 to Part I, Chapter 8 and Note 5 to Part III, Chapter 4. His first work, *The Emancipation of Massachusetts*, was a protest against the ancestor worship prevalent in New England. World War I for him fulfilled his prediction of Western civilization's collapse.

24. ***fidei defensor*** "Defender of the Faith" (Latin). One of the subsidiary titles of British monarchs.

25. ***Lincoln and Wilson*** Lincoln appropriated powers no previous president ever enjoyed. He used them to proclaim a blockade, suspend *habeus corpus* (a prisoner's right to be brought before a court to determine if his/her imprisonment is lawful), spend money without congressional authorization, imprison 18,000 Confederate sympathizers without trial, and censor the press. With laws like the Espionage Act and the Volstead Act, Mencken saw Wilson as a similar abuser of power.

26. ***Homo boobiens*** a play on Mencken's term "booboisie," the ignorant masses.

27. ***Their chief . . . shipyards*** After World War I, the affairs of veterans were in a sorry state. Many could not find jobs as employment fell nationwide. An unprecedented wave of strikes broke out—3,000 by some estimates. Here Mencken likely refers to the Seattle 1919 general strike. A state militia regiment fanned out with machine guns across the city, demanding union workers end the strike. The strike was a catastrophe, halting industrial growth in Seattle for the next 20 years.

28. ***Within a few weeks . . . hundred to one.*** See Note 5 for Part I, Chapter 5

29. ***general strike in England*** The 1926 general strike was organized to force the government to halt wage cuts and to address coal miners' grievances over working conditions.

30. ***E. W. Howe*** (1853–1937) A small-town newspaper editor, magazine publisher, and novelist. His *The Story of a Country Town* was an early example of realism in American fiction. Mencken wrote the forward to Howe's *Ventures in Common Sense.*

31. ***John D. Rockefeller*** (1839–1937). American oil magnate, philanthropist, and founder of his family fortune.

32. ***Anadyomeme*** An epithet of Aphrodite (Venus): "Rising from the sea"

33. ***McKinley*** William McKinley (1843–1901). President (R, 1897–1901).

34. ***Gompers*** Samuel Gompers (1850–1924). Union leader. His tactics and ideology were more conservative than some of his labor peers. During the war Wilson appointed Gompers to the Council of National Defense. Later he chaired a commission of labor legislation at the 1919 Peace Conference.

35. ***Walter Lippmann*** (1889–1974). One of the most influential and statesmanlike American journalists. He was a shaper of public opinion, particularly on matters of foreign policy. Lippmann admired

Mencken, calling him "the most powerful personal influence on this whole generation of educated people."

36. ***Fichte . . . existite*** Johann Gottlieb Fichte (1762–1814). German philosopher and political thinker. He was one of the founding fathers of German idealism, a movement that developed from Immanuel Kant's ethical writings. His original insights into the nature of self-awareness is evident in this quote, meaning: "It didn't exist at all."

IV. CODA

1. *The Future of Democracy*

1. ***bona fides*** Literally, "in good faith" (Latin), but used as a term referring to a person's credentials.

2. ***Holy Church*** The Roman Catholic Church.

3. ***James Bryce's "Modern Democracies"*** 1st Viscount James Bryce (1838–1922). British jurist, historian, and diplomat. Mencken reviewed Bryce's *Modern Democracies*, a study of popular governments and their workings, in the September 1921 *Smart Set.* He called it "magnificently dull." Mencken may have been biased. Bryce in 1915 chaired a committee "to Investigate Alleged German Outrages." The result, *The Bryce Report,* is now generally acknowledged as largely a tissue of unsubstantiated observations by unnamed witnesses, none of whom were put under oath or cross-examined. All documents and witness reports were destroyed at the war's end, making it impossible to verify testimony.

4. ***Lincoln's Gettysburg Address*** Lincoln's most famous speech and one of the most quoted in American history. It was delivered at the dedication of the Soldiers National Cemetery in Gettysburg, Pennsylvania, in November 1863, less than five months after a bloody battle at the same site. The speech is fewer than 300 words, yet in it Lincoln invokes the principles of equality found in the Declaration of Independence. "It is eloquence brought to a pellucid and almost gem-like perfection," wrote Mencken, with the highest emotion reduced to "a few poetical phrases. . . . It is genuinely stupendous."

However, in another piece he wrote that Lincoln in the address "stood a sentence on its head, and made a pretty parlor ornament of it. Proceeding, he described the causes and nature of the war in terms of the current army press bureau . . . Lincoln had to content himself, on a great occasion, with ideas comprehensible to Pennsylvania Drunkards, which is to say, to persons to whom genuine ideas were not comprehensible at all." (*American Mercury*, March 1928, excerpted in *Chrestomathy*, page 205.)

5. ***dogma of the Trinity*** A Christina doctrine that views God as a single Being who exists as the Father (the Source), the Son (Jesus of Nazareth), and the Holy Spirit (the Advocate). This concept has existed as "One God in three persons."

6. ***Transubstantiation*** The Roman Catholic belief that through the Eucharist the bread and wine transforms into Christ's body and blood.

7. ***Reformation*** The Protestant Reformation movement in the 16th century to reform the Catholic Church in Western Europe, started by Martin Luther (1483–1546), the German theologian.

8. ***Scholastic philosophy*** A method of instruction used in medieval universities from 1100 to 1500. It endeavored to unite Classical reason with Christianity.

9. ***New Thought*** A religious philosophy developed in the late 19th century that stresses positive thinking and mediation.

10. ***Washington Disarmament Conference*** The talks were held in Washington, D.C., from late 1921 to early 1922. Their genesis lay in the widespread fear of a naval arms race among the victorious powers of World War I: Great Britain, the U. S. and Japan. It garnered five major treaties that preserved peace in the 1920s, but it has been blamed for the rise of Japan's naval power. Mencken was booked to attend the conference, but covered it mainly from Baltimore. He was sure that Britain would outmaneuver America every time. Any pretension to "unselfishness and disinterestedness" in the conference's matters, he wrote, was a "bald fraud." ("Conference Notes," the Baltimore *Evening Sun,* November 24, 1921.*)*

11. ***Andaman Islanders*** The Andamans are a group of islands in the Bay of Bengal. The British used them as penal colony.

12. ***Great Khan*** Genghis Khan (c. 1162–1227). political and military leader, known as the "Father of Mongolia." His empire lasted more than 150 years.

13. ***vox populi, vox Dei*** "Voice of the people," "Voice of God." (Latin).

14. ***grand goblin ... grand commander*** Mencken combines Ku Klux Klan terms ("grand goblin") and fraternal titles.

15. ***Halsted*** William Stewart Halsted (1852–1922). Famous surgeon of Johns Hopkins, one of the great physicians responsible for the flowering of modern American medicine. Once again, Mencken tips his

hat to the giants of medicine and to Johns Hopkins Hospital, both of whom he held in the highest esteem.

16. ***honêtte homme*** "Honest man" (French).

17. ***Matterhorn*** Located in Switzerland, it is one of the Alps' highest peaks.

18. ***Percy or a Hohenstaufen*** This may be yet another example of Mencken's humor and outright exaggeration. "Percy" was one of England's noble families. It is also the common short form of "Percival," a Knight of the Round Table and subject of Wagner's last opera. The Hohenstaufen was a dynasty of kings of Germany, many of whom were also crowned Holy Roman Emperors and Dukes of Swabia.

2. *Last Words*

1. ***Young Intellectuals*** The juvenile highbrows and serious thinkers of the postwar generation who revolted against the contemporary life and culture of their elders. The cultural critic Harold Stearns (1891–1943) wrote of them in *America and the young intellectual* (New York: George H. Doran, 1921).

2. ***scapulae*** shoulder blades.

3. ***Jackson*** Andrew Jackson (1767–1845). President (1829–1837). Mencken refers to the Nullification Crisis (1828–1832). Jackson authorized whatever force necessary to execute laws and suppress South Carolina's nullification of federal tariffs. Another, more appalling example of Jackson's tyrannical side is the forced relocation of 18,000 to 20,000 Cherokee from their native Georgia to present-day Oklahoma. Roughly 4,000 died along "the Trail of Tears."

4. ***Cleveland*** Grover Cleveland (1837–1908). A Democrat, he served two nonconsecutive terms: 1885–1889 and 1893–1897. Mencken may be alluding to his clash with labor leader Eugene Debs. Reacting to a 25% wage cut, 50,000 Pullman railcar workers in Chicago went on strike in 1894. Cleveland refused to allow Debs to use the strike to shut down the nation's mail distribution. When the strikers persisted, Cleveland sent in 2,000 federal troops. Thirteen strikers were killed and 57 were wounded. Debs was sent to prison.

Mencken held Cleveland in great regard. Of the Pullman Strike he wrote, "Cleveland, at the start, seems to have been reluctant to intervene in Chicago, but [an adviser] convinced him that it was legal and necessary . . . It was characteristic of Cleveland that, once he had made up his mind, he struck to his course without the slightest regard for consequences . . . It is not likely that we shall see his like again, at least in the present age. The Presidency is now closed to the kind of character that he had so abundantly. It is going, in these days, to more politic and pliant men. They get it by yielding prudently, by changing their minds at the right instant, by keeping silent when speech is dangerous. Frankness and courage are luxuries confined to the more comic varieties of runners-up at national conventions . . . [Cleveland] was the last of the Romans." From the *American Mercury*, January 1933, excerpted in *Chrestomathy*, pp. 228-229.

5. ***jailed for reading the Bill of Rights*** Los Angeles police in 1923 forbade striking dockworkers from holding public gatherings. At a protest against the restriction, Upton Sinclair, author of *The Jungle*, and five others attempted to recite the First Amendment, which mandates freedom of speech and assembly. "Cut out that constitution stuff," the police admonished. After persisting, they were arrested and charged with criminal syndicalism. Following the strike, Sinclair helped to start an ACLU office in Los Angeles, the organization's first affiliate beyond its New York headquarters. (See http://www.aclu-sc.org/About/History/1923.)

6. ***a colossal swindle*** Mencken wrote that "[t]he value of this commonweal is always overestimated. What is its purpose at bottom? Simply the greatest good to the greatest number—of petty rogues, ignoramuses and chicken-hearts." (*In Defense of Women*, excerpted in *Chrestomathy*, page 29.)

Afterword

From an early age I knew about H.L. Mencken and admired him. In high school I wrote a paper based on *The American Language*. Shortly after graduating from college in 1948, I went to the Democratic National Convention of that year. There I saw Mencken in the press seats, cigar and suspenders and all. My feeling about him then was quoted by Marion Rodgers, to my amazement, in her wonderful biography, *Mencken: The American Iconoclast*. "To us," I said, "Mencken was a god."

In 1957 I wrote an article for the Harvard Law Review arguing that it was time for the Supreme Court to take up the issue of unfair legislative apportionment—the practice, followed by most state legislatures, of giving more legislative districts and hence more seats to sparsely-populated rural areas than to populous cities. I began the article with a quote from a Mencken column published in the *Evening Sun* in 1928: "The yokels hang on because old apportionments give them unfair advantages. The vote of a malarious peasant on the lower Eastern Shore counts as much as the votes of twelve Baltimoreans. But that can't last. It is not only unjust and undemocratic; it is absurd." Absurdity notwithstanding, the situation did last—until the Supreme Court changed its mind, grasped the issue, and decided in 1964 that the Equal Protection of the Laws demanded by the Constitution required equality in legislative districting.

How we could use the voice of Mencken today. He savaged Warren G. Harding as "of the intellectual grade of an aging cockroach." (Note the word "aging": It makes the insult memorable.) Just think what he would do with a president like George W. Bush, so vain and defensive that he refers to himself as "a war president" and "the decider." The only thing is that what Bush has done to our country is so much more serious than Harding's folly. He launched the war that made him "a war president"—on the basis of faulty intelligence, ignorance, and lies. He made torture an official policy of our government, something that I could not imagine would ever happen. He violated a criminal law in order to spy on Americans. His policies have cost thousands of lives and alienated most of the world.

Mencken said his aim was "to combat, chiefly by ridicule, American piety, stupidity, tin-pot morality, cheap chauvinism." I fear that the disasters suffered by his and our country in recent years are beyond ridicule. And beyond easy repair. But what a difference it would make if we had a Mencken with us to goad an altogether too timid—fawning is not too strong a word—national press.

—ANTHONY LEWIS
New York, 2007

HENRY LOUIS MENCKEN (1880–1956) was America's greatest journalist and iconoclast. With his bristling, sardonic humor and unmatched erudition, he mercilessly attacked war hysteria, Puritanism, and censorship. As a critic, he championed uniquely American writing, helping to free the nation's literature of its Anglophilia. Mencken covered many of the great stories of the twentieth century's first half, including the Scopes "Monkey" trial, Prohibition, and the New Deal. Joseph Conrad said his words emitted a "crackle of blue sparks."

MARION ELIZABETH RODGERS is the author of *Mencken: The American Iconoclast*, winner of the *ForeWord* 2005 Book of the Year Gold Award for Biography, one of *Booklist*'s "Top Ten Biographies for 2005-2006," included in *Chicago Tribune*'s Best of 2005 Nonfiction List, and a finalist for the 2005 *Los Angeles Times* Book Prize in Biography. Her previous books are *Mencken & Sara: A Life in Letters* and *The Impossible H. L. Mencken: A Selection of His Best Newspaper Stories.*

ANTHONY LEWIS is a two-time Pulitzer prize winner and former *The New York Times* columnist (1969-2001.) He currently holds the James Madison Chair of First Amendment Issues at Columbia University. He most recent book is *Freedom for the Thought That We Hate: A Biography of the First Amendment.*